Cooking Outside The Lines

MUSINGS OF AN EXTEMPERANEOUS CHEF

TO DONNA-
HERE'S TO CREATIVE
COOKING!

ALSO BY WARREN CATERSON

Table for Two – The Cookbook for Couples

Table for Two – Back for Seconds

Table for Two – The Kitchen Companion

Dive and Fly *(fiction)*

Cooking Outside The Lines

MUSINGS OF AN EXTEMPERANEOUS CHEF

WARREN CATERSON

 Winfield & Scott Press

Winfield & Scott Press
8437 Tuttle Avenue, Suite 102
Sarasota, FL 34243

Library of Congress Cataloging-in-Publication Data

Caterson, Warren.
　　　Cooking outside the lines: musings of an extemporaneous chef / Warren
　　　　　Caterson.
　　　p. cm.
　　　Includes index.
　　　LCCN 2018914091
　　　ISBN-13: 978-0-9801568-3-6
　　　ISBN-10: 0-9801568-3-1

　　　1. Cookery for two. I. Title.

TX652.C38 2009　　　　　641.5'612
　　　　　　　　　　　　　QBI08-600229

Cover Design: Rebecca Anne Russo
Author Photograph: Renee Parenteau Photography
Interior Design: BecCreative, LLC.

Printed in the United States of America

DEDICATION

To Heather, Stacy, Lindsay, Aaron and Brendan.
As you grew I watched you color outside the lines.
Man, I could learn a thing or two from each of you.

Table of Contents

TABLE OF CONTENTS CONTINUED

Preface

I had tons of coloring books when I was a kid. They were probably more prevalent back in the 50's and 60's than they are today. Back then we didn't have computers and video games.

So I had to occupy myself in more tactile ways. Maybe you did, too.

I built things with Lincoln Logs and Erector Sets.

My sister cooked imaginary meals in little pots and pans on a just-her-size stove and served them to teddy bears and baby dolls.

I staged wars with little green army men. I shot them down with rubber bands.

My sister changed diapers on baby dolls and, when she got older, she dressed Barbie and Ken.

I threw tennis balls against the wall of my house. Sometimes I threw them at my sister.

If you grew up in the 50's and 60's, I bet you did the same thing. And when we tired out from all that activity, we'd lie on the living room carpet and fish through a box of Crayola Crayons to find just the right hue to color that stark blank page of the coloring book. We took our time, making sure we didn't cross the heavy black lines of the illustration.

At least I'm sure most kids did. I didn't.

You see, I was one of the few who colored outside the lines.

And it wasn't because I suffered from a vision disorder or required medication to treat one of the popular alphabetically-designated maladies that seem to affect many of today's rambunctious kids.

No. I colored outside the lines because I felt that the lines were too restricting. In fact, more than once, I would grab a black magic marker and add additional lines to the drawing.

Then I would color outside those, too.

Of course, when I showed my finished masterpieces to the adults around me I would always hear: "That's nice, Warren. But can't you stay in the lines?"

Um. Nope.

And this quality followed me through elementary school, where I had no problem improvising during the school play. That might've flown on Saturday Night Live but it sure as heck didn't during our second grade presentation of the Wizard of Oz when I felt that my character, the Tin Man, didn't have enough funny lines.

Or in the sixth grade, when I broke out in a spontaneous song during a play that was never intended to be a musical.

Or in high school, when I often gave impassioned extemporaneous speeches at times when none were required nor desired.

Or in college when I appointed myself official sign-maker at the grocery store where I worked. (I mean, why would the produce manager get mad when he spotted an "Ask about our senior citizen discount on all poison ivy plants" in the flower section?)

I think you get my drift.

But it's who I am. And it has influenced my cooking as well.

Hopefully this little cookbook will bring a smile to you or to anyone who has the desire to color and cook outside the lines.

Because in between these pages we'll challenge conventional wisdom (searing meat seals in the juices). De-bunk age-old platitudes (place a box of baking soda in the fridge to eliminate odors.) Upend the status quo (red wine with fish? Why not?). And offer up some dishes for you to tweak (how 'bout them roasted veggies?)

And as you play around with these recipes, drop me a line if you come up with something good. I promise I'll spread the word.

Bon appétit!

P.S. In keeping with the Table for Two theme, these recipes are pretty much scaled down for two. Feel free to double or triple the ingredients for company. They'll be glad you did.

CHAPTER 1

WHY I COOK, BUT WON'T DANCE, IN PUBLIC

Why won't I dance in public?

Easy.

I'm white.

That should suffice.

Seriously, the last time I danced in public, an old man had a stroke, a cute toddler suddenly became apoplectic, and three women gave birth a month early (and one of them wasn't even pregnant).

And the last time I posted a pic on social media that even remotely looked like dancing, Savion Glover hurled his tap shoes out the window, the entire membership of the Rockettes went on a hunger strike, and a roving band of anarchists torched three Arthur Murray Studios.

I don't know about you, but I can't have things like that hanging over my head.

That's why I took dance lessons once. Every Thursday night we'd learn a new dance. Each with its own unalterable, specific steps. The waltz, merengue, foxtrot, mambo, swing, etc. Which was great. Except for those of us who are memory-challenged. I couldn't remember what I learned from week to week, let alone retain it for a lifetime.

Heck, my memory is so bad I can't remember what I wrote in the previous paragraph.

A good dancer not only remembers the steps, he or she is so comfortable with their talent they feel free to improvise. And it works.

There's something about cooking that stays with me. I'm comfortable with it. Which is why I'm more than glad to cook in public.

After all, no one's hurled their kitchen gear out the window, there've been no early births, cute toddlers remain cute toddlers, and almost no one has died of a stroke.

So I cook. And the more I cook, the more I cook outside the lines. Just like a good dancer.

Hopefully this book will help you cook outside the lines, too.

First item on the menu is a recipe I gleaned from Doc Ford's Rum Bar & Grill on Sanibel Island. There are a number of recipes for this floating out there on the web, but I think this is the version closest to what is recognized as their signature dish. In keeping with our theme, I'm offering up several ways to prepare it.

Shall we get started?

• TRADITIONAL YUCATAN SHRIMP •

With 1-pound of shrimp, this lightning-quick dish for two could almost double as a light soup. Whenever you pine for an evening in the islands, whip up a pot of this, warm some bread, pour a cold beverage of choice, then snuggle up and stream "South Pacific" from Netflix.

PREP: 5 minutes   COOK: 10 minutes

INGREDIENTS
  1 pound large or extra-large, shell-on shrimp *(for a special treat, look for Argentinean Reds)*

  4 tablespoons unsalted butter, divided

  1 large clove garlic, minced or pressed

  Juice of two large limes

  1 tablespoon Sambal Oelek
  (This is a ground fresh chili paste made by Hu Fong Foods, the company that wowed the culinary world with their Sriracha Sauce. It can be found in just about any grocery store in the Oriental food isle. Just look for the red rooster on the label).

  Kosher salt and freshly ground black pepper to taste

  2 tablespoons chopped fresh cilantro

DIRECTIONS
  1. Melt 1 tablespoon butter in a small saucepan over medium heat. Add the garlic and cook, stirring until fragrant, about 1 or 2 minutes (do not brown). Add remaining 3 tablespoons butter to saucepan. When melted, stir in the lime juice, chili paste, salt and pepper. Turn off the heat and let the sauce to rest to allow the flavors to meld.

  2. Meanwhile, bring a large pot of well-salted water to a boil. Add the shrimp and cook for 2 minutes or until they're just firm and pink. Please don't over cook - no one likes to eat little pink hockey pucks! Drain the shrimp in a colander and shake over the sink to remove excess moisture.

  3. Toss the shrimp with the sauce in a large bowl. Sprinkle with cilantro and toss again. Serve in shallow bowls with an ice cold brew, plenty of napkins, crusty bread and a salad.

• YUCATAN SHRIMP ON THE GRILL •

Use the same ingredients as above and follow step one. Keep sauce warm while you grill the shrimp.

Prepare an outdoor grill for medium-high heat. Place the shrimp on skewers (I alternate them - like the I-Ching symbol) so they are very close together. They'll be less likely to dry out that way. Oil grate and grill shrimp, turning once or twice until they just turn pink. Toss with the sauce and cilantro in a large bowl.

• PAN-SEARED YUCATAN SHRIMP •

Decrease the chili paste to 1/2 or 3/4 tablespoons because the shrimp will absorb more of the sauce without the shells.

DIRECTIONS
1. Heat a 10-inch skillet over medium-high heat. Add 1 tablespoon butter and swirl to coat the pan. Add the garlic and sauté for about 1 minute.

2. Add the shrimp and sauté until just turning pink, about 2 -3 minutes. Stir in the remaining butter, lime juice, chili paste, salt and pepper and continue to sauté until shrimp are just barely firm. Pour the shrimp and sauce into a large bowl. Sprinkle with cilantro and toss. Serve in shallow bowls.

CHAPTER 2

10 NEW YEAR'S FOOD RESOLUTIONS EVERYONE SHOULD MAKE

Eat more fruits and vegetables. Studies from the American Heart Association show that a diet high in fruits and vegetables may result in a higher ingestion of fruits and vegetables. This, I'm assuming, is probably a good thing. Unless, of course, you happen to be a carrot or a pineapple. (Or heaven forbid, a tomato. At which point you may lose out on both counts.)

Never order anything off the menu that says "Big Ass." Restaurant menu choices that use the qualifier "Big Ass" are, in all probability, not good choices for a healthy lifestyle. This includes such popular crowd-pleasing items as Burger Gem's *"Big Ass Bacon Swiss Mushroom Burger"*, Pizza Time's *"Big Ass Meat-Lovers Three-Cheese Pizza"*, and Le Bernardin's *"Big Ass Caviar Wagyu with Black Pepper-Vodka Crème Frâiche and Pomme Gaufrette."*

Don't wear raw meat. Even though Lady Gaga pulled it off at the MTV Video Awards a few years ago, wearing raw meat as a fashion statement is not going to win over many fans. Unless, of course, you're courting the canine constituency of music industry voters. I haven't seen so many Dobermans hovering around an awards show since Gary Coleman wore that fire hydrant outfit to the Golden Globes back in '97. (Memo to self: Return the pepperoni socks that you bought yourself for Christmas from Don's Fresh Meats and Western Haberdashery.)

Buy organic. A recent article in the *National Journal of Health* suggests that those who eat organically tend to live not only healthier lives but happier ones as well. Therefore, they strongly recommend that we should all be more organic. No, wait. I thought that said orgasmic. Never mind.

Cut back on salt. Yes, I know you love salt; we all do. But as you get older you'll need to cut back. So for goodness sake, regardless of how strong the urge is, try to refrain from getting down on your hands and knees and licking the salt off the sidewalks this winter.

Buy local. Hopping in the old sedan and driving out to Omaha to pick up some nice ribeyes, or across country to Salinas Valley in California to pick up a few heads of lettuce is not only time intensive, but considering the cost of gasoline, it may not be economically feasible, either. You should buy all these items down at your local farmers' market.

Eat more garlic. Studies over the past decade or two show that people who eat garlic every day have lower incidences of cancer and heart disease. However, a 2012 study by the Lucy Berkoff Medical Foundation also shows that people who do so are usually forced to sit by themselves in most social situations. Since my twisted sense of humor usually forces me to sit by myself in most social situations anyway, eating garlic on a daily basis was a no-brainer.

Save the bones for Henry Jones 'cuz Henry don't eat no meat. I learned this little ditty growing up outside New York City in the early 60's. It was sound wisdom then, and it is sound wisdom now. I mean, what else are you planning to do with your leftover bones? Besides, I hear that old man Henry makes some killer soup stock.

If you can't pronounce it, lift it or describe it, don't eat it. Here's a 3-in-1 tidbit of advice. When you pick up a package at the grocery store, look at the ingredients. If there's anything listed that you can't pronounce, pass on it. The same goes for any package you have trouble picking up. Even if you use both hands. And if you can't describe what you're eating beyond something akin to, "It sorta tastes kinda like what I thought I ate last Saturday…or was that Friday?" you probably shouldn't take another bite.

Drink more water. The Mayo Clinic suggests that we strive to drink at least 6 eight-ounce glasses of water each day for optimal health. The International Whisky Society suggests that we strive to mix that water with a decent scotch for optimal taste.

CHAPTER 3

WHEN GIVING UP IS GOOD

Now that I've got a couple of books in print, there are two things I've learned about myself in regard to computers, technology, and publishing:

One: I'm an idiot

Two: I'm an idiot.

At first I was frustrated with my lack of knowledge and talent. I even ordered a slew of books on publishing, Website design, e-communications, search engine optimization, blah blah blah. And yet, after all that study, I find I'm just as clueless as I was before I helped Amazon CEO Jeff Bezos take one more step to becoming a gazillionaire. Except now, after buying all these books, I have a really good supply of doorstops. Anyway, since I had neither the time, talent nor inclination to become a tech whiz, I did the next best thing. I cracked open a can of Pabst Blue Ribbon, took a seat on the porch, and gave up.

That's right.

I gave up.

The tech part that is.

Yep. I gave it up to folks who know what they're doing. I have a wonderful friend, Melanie, who helps with Facebook and Twitter. Cathy helps me with my webpage. Becky's cover art never ceases to amaze me. Renee Parenteau's awesome photography (which reminds me, I have to set up another shoot with her). And the good folks at MailChimp and Less Annoying CRM for helping to keep my communications flowing smoothly.

Without friends like these, I might still be pouring over books I don't understand instead of testing a new recipe someone sent in, engaging folk at a food & wine festival, or writing a new book. These are things I'm told I'm good at, and certainly things I enjoy. I once heard a motivational speaker proclaim, "Never give up!" Baloney. Sometimes it's good to give up. I'm glad I did.

Is there something that you need to give up? Something someone else could do better, so you can concentrate on what you do well? I'm sure there is. Find that someone and let them have at it. Lord knows there are enough doorstops in this world. While we're thinking of those jobs that are best left to others, why don't we whip up some pita pizzas, okay?

• PERSONAL PAN PIZZAS •
(Okay, Not in a Pan, But Close)

I like to occasionally order out for pizza, especially if one of the local joints is running a special. Since they do pizza so well, I have no problem with take out. But there are times when I want something a little bit different, something they don't offer. Oh, and I want it super fast. Then I'll make my own. Like these personal pita pizzas.

BASIC PITA PIZZA

PREP: 5 minutes   COOK: 8 minutes

INGREDIENTS
   2 pita bread rounds (or 2 English muffins, split and lightly toasted)
   1/2 cup good quality tomato sauce or pizza sauce, divided
   1/2 cup grated mozzarella or Monterey jack cheese, divided
   Favorite pizza toppings: pepperoni, cooked sausage, olives, peppers, anchovies, etc.

DIRECTIONS
   1. Place oven rack on lower 1/3 of the oven. Preheat oven or toaster oven to 400°.

   2. Place pita rounds on a baking sheet or pizza stone. Spread 1/4 cup sauce over each pita then sprinkle with 1/4 cup shredded cheese. Add additional toppings if desired.

   3. Bake until cheese is bubbly and slightly brown, about 6 to 8 minutes. Serve immediately.

GARLICKY SHRIMP PIZZA

INGREDIENTS

   2 pita bread rounds (or 2 English muffins, split and lightly toasted)

   12 large shrimp, peeled and deveined re

   4 cloves garlic, crushed

   2 tablespoons olive oil

   1/2 cup grated mozzarella cheese, divided

   1/2 cup grated fontina, gruyere or swiss cheese, divided

   1 ounce goat or feta cheese, chunked and divided

   1 tablespoon grated Parmesan cheese, divided

   2 tablespoons chopped red or yellow pepper (or jarred pimento), divided

   1/2 cup halved cherry tomatoes, divided

DIRECTIONS

1. Place oven rack on lower 1/3 of the oven. Preheat oven or toaster oven to 400°.

2. Meanwhile, heat olive oil in a 10-inch skillet over medium heat. Add garlic and sauté until fragrant and gold, about 2 minutes. Add shrimp and sauté until they just turn pink, about 3 or 4 minutes. Remove shrimp with a slotted spoon and reserve oil.

3. Place pita rounds on a baking sheet or pizza stone and sprinkle half the mozzarella and fontina cheese on each pita. Arrange half the shrimp and half the goat cheese. Add half the cherry tomatoes and sprinkle with half of the Parmesan cheese. Drizzle with reserved garlic oil.

4. Bake until cheese is bubbly and slightly brown, about 6 to 8 minutes. Serve immediately.

NEW YORK REUBEN PIZZA

INGREDIENTS
  2 pita bread rounds (or 2 English muffins, split and lightly toasted)
  1/4 cup thousand island dressing, divided
  1 cup shredded Swiss cheese, divided
  1/4 pound deli sliced corned beef, cut into strips, divided
  1/2 cup sauerkraut, rinsed and drained, divided
  1/4 teaspoon caraway seed, divided
  2 tablespoons chopped dill pickles, divided (optional)

DIRECTIONS
  1. Place oven rack on lower 1/3 of the oven. Preheat oven or toaster oven to 400°.

  2. Place pita rounds on a baking sheet or pizza stone. Spread 1 tablespoon of the salad dressing on each pita. Sprinkle with 1/4 -cup of the Swiss cheese. Arrange corned beef over the cheese, then drizzle with the remaining salad dressing. Top with sauerkraut and remaining Swiss cheese. Sprinkle with caraway seeds.

  3. Bake until cheese is bubbly and slightly brown, about 6 to 8 minutes. Sprinkle with chopped pickle. Let stand for 5 minutes before slicing.

MARGHERITA PIZZA

INGREDIENTS
2 pita bread rounds (or 2 English muffins, split and lightly toasted)

3/4 cup chopped tomatoes, drained, divided (you can used canned)

1/2 cup shredded mozzarella cheese, divided

2 garlic cloves, crushed, divided

4 fresh basil leaves, cut into strips, divided

2 tablespoons grated Parmesan cheese

1 tablespoon olive oil, divided

DIRECTIONS
1. Place oven rack on lower 1/3 of the oven. Preheat oven or toaster oven to 400°.

2. Place pita rounds on a baking sheet or pizza stone. Spoon half of the tomatoes on each pita. Season with salt and pepper to taste. Sprinkle each with half the garlic and mozzarella cheese. Spread the basil leaves over the top, sprinkle with half the Parmesan cheese, then drizzle with olive oil.

3. Bake until cheese is bubbly and slightly brown, about 6 to 8 minutes. Serve immediately.

CHAPTER 4

DIETS I HAVE TRIED THAT REALLY DO WORK

One of the major traditions of every New Year is our penchant to lose weight, and hence, our adoption of the latest 'fad' diet.

A national magazine recently posted a list of diets that are not only ineffective, but may actually be hazardous to our health. For instance, there's the infamous the "Breatharian Diet", which insists that we get all of our sustenance through the simple act of breathing.

While I thought this article beneficial, I felt that the world has had enough of 'diets that won't work'. So I thought that I'd share a list of diets I've tried that actually do work:

The "Information Diet". Unlike the Breatharian Diet mentioned above, on this diet one thrives on ideas. I've been on this diet since kindergarten. And here's the funny thing: even though my brain has gotten bigger, I haven't gained that much weight. Perhaps if we all focused more on our minds and less on our stomachs, we might be better off. Hey...it's just an idea...

The "Don't Eat Anything You Can Eat While Driving Diet". Good meals are meant to be eaten while sitting down, but not while sitting down behind the wheel of a car. If we can eat something while weaving in and out of traffic, we might do well to pass on it.

The "Only Drink Alcohol on Days that End in "Y" Diet". Studies show that although moderate alcohol consumption provides some healthy heart benefits they're also loaded with empty calories. So if one wants to lose weight, one should limit their alcohol intake. This is why I only drink on days that end in the letter "Y". I perfected this diet back when I figured out how to use a corkscrew. What can I say? I'm part Irish.

The "Miss Piggy Diet" (or "The Don't Eat Anything You Can't Lift Diet)". I thought this would be a no-brainer until I saw a semi-truck hauling cattle sideswipe a tour bus hauling folks to a timeshare lecture near Orlando. The semi then careened into a bridge abutment and burst into flames. As I pulled to the shoulder, 52 tourists in Hawaiian shirts, Bermuda shorts and flowery sundresses spilled out of the bus and converged on the burning cattle car. I watched in amazement as they dragged whole sides of beef into the median and had themselves one heck of a picnic. But note, they dragged the beef. No one lifted anything.

The "If You Can't Pronounce It, Don't Eat It Diet". The next time you're tempted to pick up a prepackaged convenience meal at the grocery store, read the ingredients. If you find something listed that you can't pronounce, don't eat it.

The "Sounds Like a High School Chemistry Class Assignment Diet". And if you find an ingredient that sounds like it came out of a high school chemistry book, pass on it. (See above.)

The "Grocery Store Perimeter Diet". First popularized by author Michael Pollan, this diet consists of eating mostly those things found on the perimeter aisles of the grocery store (along with the occasional foray down the frozen food aisle to snatch up some plain frozen veggies).

The "If Paula Deen Made It, Screw It Diet". Okay, although I was not born in the South, I now live in the South. And I love a lot of southern cooking. But one must draw the line. So let's draw it here. Hey, it's a start.

The "Fuppie Diet". Back in the 80's, the word Yuppie was coined to denote that cultural phenomena known as Young Urban Professionals. Soon after, the word Buppie was coined, denoting Black Urban Professionals. That's when I decided the world needed Fuppies. Folks like me who just don't give a fup. Especially when it comes to fad diets. Who's with me?

CHAPTER 5

SUPER BOWL SUNDAY REDUX AND A KILLER STEW

Back in 2005, Jacksonville, Florida hosted the Super Bowl. I imagine the intent was to show off the city, and, as a result, attract a bevy of business suitors and new residents. They spent a lot of time and money sprucing up downtown, but doing so was like a friend showing off her newly-shaved armpits. Sure, they might look better than they did before, but they are still armpits.

The Friday before the big event, I bundled up to go for a walk at lunch. It was too cold to stroll the Riverwalk. The temperature was rapidly falling. Bone chill. The air so brittle I could almost hear it cracking as I moved forward. This was a typical deep-winter day in Northeast Florida. It was much more forgiving than her New England cousin, but the frigid wind blowing in off the ocean seemed to tease me as it sneered, "Welcome to the Sunshine State."

Flashback: Chicago, 2000. Jerry and I trudging through Old Town in mid-February. Ash-gray snow piled high on the curbs. Luminescent halos surrounding the streetlights. We're hunched over; challenging a wind that seemed determined to keep us walking in place.

It's nearly 11 PM when we push open the doors to the Second City Comedy Club and shake off the bitter cold. We join our party in the upstairs lobby where handshakes and hugs flow freely. A loud "thunk", like that of a human body striking steel, draws our attention. We turn to see a drunk-to-the-gills college student trying to navigate his way down the curved iron stairway. He falls again amid the roar of laughter from several dozen bystanders. He grasps the banister like a pole-vaulter grabs his pole and hoists himself back up, only to tumble down a few more steps. Obviously thinking the better of it, he opts to crawl the rest of the way down. Perhaps some Good Samaritan should let him know when he gets to the bottom. I almost volunteer, but the show is about to start.

Jump Cut: I'm back in Jacksonville continuing my stroll. I'm waiting for the light when a blonde and curvaceous woman appeared beside me and asked directions to an ATM machine.

I almost pointed out the nearest one.

Instead, I nodded at a tall building in the distance and said, "I think there's one at the bank." We walked for blocks, engaged in good conversation and laughter. The wind picked up and she slipped her arm in mine. She told me that she just relocated to the area after a messy divorce and recently completed massage therapy school.

She now works at a Chevy dealership on the Westside giving massages to people as they waited for their cars to be fixed. Who knew such jobs existed? I thought about my 12-year old car and decided that's where I'm going to start taking it for repairs.

We finally came to a teller machine and said goodbye. She thanked me with a kiss on the cheek and turned to walk away. As I watched her skip across Julia Street, I wondered what she'd think when she passes some ATMs on her return trip. Somehow, I didn't think she'd mind.

I turned up Laura Street to see a crowd of people gathered at the park. I wandered over and worked my way in to get a better look at what everyone else was watching. In the center of the park, a group of big burly guys moved in a way that could only be described as Tai Chi. The crowd watched in wonder as these monstrous men went through their synchronized routine without missing a beat. I nudged the guy next to me and said, "I've read about pro football players learning ballet, but this is the first time I've seen them take up Tai Chi." The man turned and squinted, "What do you mean, Tai Chi? They ain't doing Tai Chi. They're rehearsing slow motion replays for the big game."

I wiggled my way out of the crowd and headed over to The Landing, Jacksonville's ode to New Urbanism. This riverfront mall opened in the 80's to revitalize downtown. High-end shops like Banana Republic, the Sharper Image, and Coach moved in with great fanfare, only to move out a year later with barely a whisper. It seemed that everyone involved in the project was so giddy and enthusiastic that they forgot to include a parking lot in the master plan. A few restaurants have survived serving the downtown lunch crowd, but save for a teenage clothing store and knick-knack shop, most of the storefronts sit empty. Until Super Bowl week. Since we were the hosts, the Landing was packed, and it seemed that every vacant space had been turned into a temporary Super Bowl store filled with officially licensed NFL paraphernalia - which meant that $100 team jackets could now sell for $500. I decided to hold out for the unofficially unlicensed gear; creative entrepreneurs would be hawking them out of car trunks down near La Villa and Brooklyn.

I left the warmth of the Landing and made my way up Main toward my office when the sounds of blaring sirens grabbed my attention. I turned to see the Patriots coming across the Main Street Bridge. A half-dozen black limos and two Greyhound buses were chasing some unseen rabbit, flanked fore and aft by motorcycle cops, their sirens screaming and lights flashing.

Overhead, two police helicopters hovered and dipped. The sound shook the ground and rattled the windows of the surrounding buildings. A homeless man approached, pushing a Winn Dixie cart filled with aluminum cans. "Hell," he said as he passed. "They're just football players not the goddam second coming." I nodded in agreement and it looked like he enjoyed this brief moment of camaraderie.

I headed north then turned east onto Church Street where I noticed a freshly poured concrete sidewalk and I'm suddenly nine years old again. I glanced around. Not a soul in sight. I stepped forward and heard a slight crunch under my soles. I started to walk, my wingtips leaving gentle imprints. I turned, smiled, and admired my handiwork. I bent down, pulled a pen from my jacket pocket, and etched my initials in the gray ooze next to my footprints. My legacy for the ages, stamped in concrete, and more permanent than the random thoughts I commit to paper.

Well, it's one legacy. The other is this Super Bowl Sunday Stew. This recipe will serve way more than two because it's just too good not to share.

• SUPER BOWL SUNDAY STEW •

Start this around noon and it'll be ready for the big game. I'm making this with beef, but I've also made it with venison (thanks, Rusty!).

PREP: 20 minutes   COOK: 1 hour

INGREDIENTS

1-1/2 pound chuck roast, trimmed of fat and cut into 1-inch cubes

1 tablespoon olive or canola oil

1 medium onion, chopped

5 stalks celery, diced (include the leaves)

3 or 4 cloves of garlic, minced or pressed

6 tablespoons unsalted butter

1/3 cup all-purpose flour

3 carrots, peeled and sliced thin

4 teaspoons beef base (Tones®, Better than Bouillon®, Minors®, etc)

1 32-oz bottle tomato or V8 Juice® (I use V8 'cuz we always have it on hand)

1 28-oz can chopped tomatoes

1 bay leaf

1 tablespoon olive or canola oil

1-1/2 teaspoons soy sauce

2 medium-sized red or Yukon gold potatoes, diced Kosher salt and freshly ground pepper to taste

DIRECTIONS

1. Heat the olive oil in a 10-inch skillet over medium-high heat. Add the onions and celery and sauté until onions are soft, about 8 minutes. Add the garlic and sauté an additional 1 to 2 minutes. Pour vegetables into a small bowl and set aside.

2. Melt the butter in a dutch oven over medium-high heat. Add the flour and stir constantly to make a smooth paste and begins to turn tan, about 3 to 5 minutes. Slowly pour in the tomato or V8 juice. Stir until smooth and slightly thickened. Add the beef base and stir to dissolve. Bring to a boil and add the onion/celery mixture, carrots, tomatoes and bay leaf. Return to a boil, lower heat, and simmer covered for about 30 minutes.

3. In the meantime, heat the olive or canola oil in the 10-inch skillet over medium-high heat. Add the beef in batches and sauté until brown. Drain the meat and set aside. Deglaze the pan with a little beef broth or red wine to dissolve the brown bits on the bottom of the pan. Add this to the meat.

4. When the vegetables have simmered for 30 minutes, add the beef and Kitchen Bouquet and simmer for 1 hour. Add the potatoes and simmer an additional 20 minutes or until potatoes are tender. Taste for salt (you may not need much depending on how much salt is in the tomato/V8 juice).

Serve with lots of crusty bread.

COOKING OUTSIDE THE LINES VARIATIONS

In lieu of beef, substitute:

1-1/2 pounds cubed boneless, skinless chicken thighs

1-1/2 pounds cubed pork loin

1-1/2 pounds cubed lamb shoulder

2 cans red or white or beans

CHAPTER 6

THE WORST VALENTINE'S DAY GIFT EVER

Whenever I do cooking demonstrations someone always asks if I'm a chef in a restaurant.

I always tell them no.

The restaurant business is tough when you have a family. Long hours. Lot's of late nights. Working the holidays. You get the drift. And although I now love to cook, I never was inspired to do so when I was in my teens. In fact, the impetus to cook came about through what might be described as the worst Valentine's gift ever.

My wife and I had been married for a number of years when one of my young daughters called me at work to ask what I'd gotten Mom for Valentine's Day. I froze. I had forgotten. "Something nice," I reassured her. Then I hung up the phone and raced to the mall.

Okay. I was in a panic. I wasn't thinking straight when I stumbled into a Waldenbooks store and frantically scanned the shelves. My eyes fell on a gourmet cookbook. That's it! I smiled and snatched it off the shelf. I even had the clerk gift wrap it for me.

At home, after dinner and when the kids had all presented their homemade Valentine's Day cards to my wife and me, my wife handed me my gift, an envelope. I opened it and found a gift certificate for a free massage at a local spa. "Because", she said," You work so hard."

I gulped.

Then handed her my gift.

She felt the heft and I'm sure she thought it was some serious jewelry. She gingerly unwrapped it and held the cookbook in her hands. Time seemed to stop.

"A cookbook?" she asked without looking up.

I knew I was screwed. I woulda been better off buying her an iron or a vacuum cleaner.

"Do you like it?" I asked. "It's gourmet."

She glanced up and said, "You're lucky to get what I make with all these kids pining for my attention, Buster."

I gulped again. My mind raced. Then I blurted out, "The cookbook's not for you. It's for me!"

Her eyebrows scrunched up into "please-explain-mode".

"See," I continued. "I'm going to cook you a gourmet meal this Friday. We'll put the kids to bed, open a bottle of wine and feast on a meal that will be fit for the gods."

At that, tears filled her eyes and she hugged me like there was no tomorrow. She smothered me in kisses and later that night we made passionate love.

My only regret? I wish I had bought her a cookbook years ago.

So that Friday, I cracked open the book and cooked up a meal. It came out great. And I enjoyed cooking it.

So I began cooking out of the book every Friday night. Then I bought some more books and began cooking every Thursday and Friday night. Soon I was cooking every night of the week.

I'd like to say it was all altruistic but the truth was, I was doing inner-city youth work at the time and some days were pretty intense. So coming home and pouring a glass of wine while I labored over a delicious meal was actually relaxing for me.

Here are some recipes from the Provence - Cote d'Azur region of France that I always enjoying making this time of year. These are not 'haute cuisine' recipes, but I think you'll find these savory, fresh and healthy 'variations on a theme' perfect for a romantic dinner.

An added plus? You won't spend a lot of time hovering over a hot stove.

The recipes, as you'll see, are very similar. Learn to make one and you'll find yourself making them all. And as always, feel free to tweak based on what's in season.

• TUNA PROVENÇAL •

PREP: 10 minutes   COOK: 10 minutes

INGREDENTS

2 tuna steaks

Kosher salt and fresh ground pepper to taste

2 tablespoons olive oil, divided

1 large shallot (or 1 scallion) chopped

Pinch of dried red pepper, or to taste

2 plum tomatoes, chopped (or 2/3 cup canned chopped tomatoes)

1/3 cup chopped Kalamata olives

1/4 cup chopped fresh basil, divided

1 tablespoon capers, drained

3 tablespoons clam juice (or chicken broth)

3 tablespoons dry white wine

DIRECTIONS

1. Season tuna with salt and pepper to taste. Heat a 10-inch skillet over medium-high heat. Add 1 tablespoon oil and swirl to coat Add tuna and cook until nicely brown but still medium-rare in the center, about 3 minutes per side. Transfer tuna to a plate and cover.

2   Add remaining oil to the skillet and swirl to coat. Add shallots and red pepper and sauté for 1 minute. Stir in tomatoes, olives, 2 tablespoons basil, and capers; sauté 1 minute. Stir in the clam juice and white wine. Boil until sauce slightly thickens, about 4 minutes. Stir in remaining basil and spoon over tuna.

Serve over steamed white rice, couscous or quinoa.

• CHICKEN PROVENÇAL •

PREP: 10 minutes   COOK: 15 minutes

INGREDENTS
  2 boneless, skinless chicken breasts, pounded to 1/2 – 1/4 inch thick
  Kosher salt and fresh ground pepper to taste
  2 tablespoons olive oil, divided
  1 large shallot (or 1 scallion) chopped
  Pinch of dried red pepper, or to taste
  2 plum tomatoes, chopped (or 2/3 cup canned chopped tomatoes)
  1/3 cup chopped Kalamata olives
  1/4 cup chopped fresh basil, divided
  1 tablespoon capers, drained
  3 tablespoons chicken broth
  3 tablespoons dry white wine

DIRECTIONS
  1   Season chicken with salt and pepper to taste. Heat a 10-inch skillet over
       medium-high heat. Add 1 tablespoon oil and swirl to coat Add chicken and
       cook until nicely brown, about 3 minutes per side. Transfer chicken to a plate
       and cover.

  2.   Add remaining oil to the skillet and swirl to coat. Add shallots and red pepper
       and sauté for 1 minute. Stir in tomatoes, olives, 2 tablespoons basil, and
       capers; sauté 1 minute. Stir in the chicken broth and white wine. Return
       chicken to the pan. Boil until sauce slightly thickens, about 4 minutes. Stir in
       remaining basil and spoon over chicken.

Serve over steamed white rice, couscous or quinoa.

• BEEF PROVENÇAL •

PREP: 10 minutes   COOK: 15 minutes

INGREDENTS
  6 – 8 ounce flat iron or flank steak
  Kosher salt and fresh ground pepper to taste
  1 tablespoon olive oil
  1 large shallot (or 1 scallion) chopped
  Pinch of dried red pepper, or to taste
  2 plum tomatoes, chopped (or 2/3 cup canned chopped tomatoes)
  1/3 cup chopped Kalamata olives
  1/4 cup chopped fresh basil, divided
  1 tablespoon capers, drained
  3 tablespoons beef broth
  3 tablespoons dry white wine

DIRECTIONS
  1. Season steak with salt and pepper to taste. Pre-heat your gas or charcoal
      grill for medium-high. Lightly oil grate. Place the steak on the grill and cook
      about 3 – 4 minutes per side for medium-rare. Transfer steak to a plate,
      cover and let rest for 5 minutes.

  2. Meanwhile, add oil to a 10-inch skillet and swirl to coat. Add shallots and red
      pepper and sauté for 1 minute. Stir in tomatoes, olives, 2 tablespoons basil,
      and capers; sauté 1 minute. Stir in the beef broth and white wine. Boil until
      sauce slightly thickens, about 4 minutes. Stir in remaining basil. Slice into 1/2
      – inch thick slices across the grain and spoon sauce over slices.

Serve over steamed white rice, couscous or quinoa.

• PORK PROVENÇAL •

PREP: 10 minutes   COOK: 15 minutes

INGREDENTS
  3/4 pound pork tenderloin, cut crosswise into 8 medallions

  Kosher salt and fresh ground pepper to taste

  2 tablespoons olive oil, divided

  1 large shallot (or 1 scallion) chopped

  Pinch of dried red pepper, or to taste

  2 plum tomatoes, chopped (or 2/3 cup canned chopped tomatoes)

  1/3 cup chopped Kalamata olives

  1/4 cup chopped fresh basil, divided

  1 tablespoon capers, drained

  3 tablespoons chicken broth

  3 tablespoons dry white wine

DIRECTIONS
  1. Arrange pork medallions in a single layer on a work surface, and press each
      with the palm of your hand to flatten to an even thickness. Season with salt
      and pepper to taste. Heat a 10-inch skillet over medium-high heat. Add 1
      tablespoon oil and swirl to coat Add pork and cook until nicely brown but still
      medium-rare in the center, about 3 minutes per side. Transfer pork to a plate
      and cover.

  2. Add remaining oil to the skillet and swirl to coat. Add shallots and red pepper
      and sauté for 1 minute. Stir in tomatoes, olives, 2 tablespoons basil, and
      capers; sauté 1 minute. Stir in the chicken broth and white wine. Boil until
      sauce slightly thickens, about 4 minutes. Stir in remaining basil and spoon
      over pork.

Serve over steamed white rice, couscous or quinoa.

• LAMB PROVENÇAL •

PREP: 10 minutes   COOK: 10 minutes

INGREDENTS
  4 3-ounce lamb chops
  Kosher salt and fresh ground pepper to taste
  2 tablespoons olive oil, divided
  1 large shallot (or 1 scallion) chopped
  Pinch of dried red pepper, or to taste
  2 plum tomatoes, chopped (or 2/3 cup canned chopped tomatoes)
  1/3 cup chopped Kalamata olives
  1/4 cup chopped fresh basil, divided
  1 tablespoon capers, drained
  3 tablespoons chicken broth
  3 tablespoons dry white wine

DIRECTIONS
  1. Season lamb with salt and pepper to taste. Heat a 10-inch skillet over
      medium-high heat. Add 1 tablespoon oil and swirl to coat Add chops and
      cook until nicely brown but still medium-rare in the center, about 3 minutes
      per side. Transfer lamb to a plate and cover.

  2. Add remaining oil to the skillet and swirl to coat. Add shallots and red pepper
      and sauté for 1 minute. Stir in tomatoes, olives, 2 tablespoons basil, and
      capers; sauté 1 minute. Stir in the chicken broth and white wine. Boil until
      sauce slightly thickens, about 4 minutes. Stir in remaining basil and spoon
      over lamb.

Serve over steamed white rice, couscous or quinoa.

• PASTA PROVENÇAL •
(Vegetarian)

PREP: 10 minutes   COOK: 10 minutes

INGREDIENTS

Prepare 6 – 8 ounces rotini, shells, or penne pasta

1 tablespoons olive oil

1 large shallot (or 1 scallion) chopped

Pinch of dried red pepper, or to taste

2 plum tomatoes, chopped (or 2/3 cup canned chopped tomatoes)

1/3 cup chopped Kalamata olives

1/4 cup chopped fresh basil, divided

1 tablespoon capers, drained

3 tablespoons vegetable broth

3 tablespoons dry white wine

DIRECTIONS

1. Prepare pasta according to directions on the box.

2. Meanwhile, Add oil to the skillet and swirl to coat. Add shallots and red pepper and sauté for 1 minute. Stir in tomatoes, olives, 2 tablespoons basil, and capers; sauté 1 minute. Stir in the clam juice and white wine. Boil until sauce slightly thickens, about 4 minutes. Stir in remaining basil and spoon over pasta.

CHAPTER 7

THE BEST ADVICE IS ALWAYS FREE
(OR: WHY I LOVE MY JOB)

I just came off a weeklong book-and-cooking tour on the west coast of Florida. For those of you who have never been, the west coast of Florida is similar to the west coast of California in that the sunsets, the beaches, and the women are gorgeous. It's unlike the west coast of California in that most of the people who should be in institutions are already there.

One of the pleasures of touring is getting to meet so many different and wonderful people. Whether I'm sautéing shrimp under a tent in 95-degree heat for a crowd or cooking up chicken marsala in a comfortable waterfront home for a dozen new friends, I always enjoy this aspect of making my way in the world as a cookbook author.

Of course another added benefit is hearing about new places to eat and new ways to cook.

For instance, when I was in Tampa, Bill told me about a killer mobile eatery called, appropriately, The Taco Bus. I also found out about a restaurant called The Refinery. It features locally grown ingredients served up with a bit of panache minus the attitude. Both of these are on my list for a visit the next time I'm in town. There's a new tea shop down near Davis Island that I'm dying to visit, and of course there's always Kelly's in downtown Dunedin. My visits there would be incomplete if I didn't stop at Kelly's at least once for breakfast.

I also met Chef John at one of my favorite after-work attitude-adjustment emporiums. He also wrote a cookbook, and we spent a good bit of time discussing the possibility of hosting a food event in the area. I'll keep you informed.

And then there are always the simple suggestions and advice that flow between folks who have something in common (food) and are having a good time (festivals). Here are a few that I filed away in that part of my brain called "Good Ideas." Some are mine. Most I gleaned from others:

For perfect pasta, make sure you boil the water before adding the pasta. (Thanks, Brendan.)

Don't try to sharpen a knife after three or four margaritas. (Thanks, Ron.)

Cooking food at a food festival will help sell more cookbooks. However, cooking up the birds you ran over in the festival parking lot will not. (Thanks, Gina.)

Don't try to sell your books while wearing a wife-beater t-shirt. This is true for cookbooks but it's especially true for children's books. I recently witnessed a guy in a wife-beater shirt selling children's books at an outdoor market a few weeks back. If you want to see parents grab their kids and drag them to the opposite end of the market, just wear a wife-beater t-shirt.

Buying the absolute cheapest of anything will never save you time (or money) in the long run. This goes for chef's knives, cookware, and unidentifiable, yet creatively named, items in the meat department. (Thanks, Randy.)

Make sure the beater blades on your mixer have completely stopped before you attempt to lick the icing off them. (Thanks, Sheila.)

Growing your own herbs is both healthy and frugal. Growing them where your dog decides to relieve herself is not. (Thanks, Megan.)

Don't fry bacon naked. (Thanks, Dan.)

And finally:

Tossing around ideas and suggestions with friends is a great way to spend the evening. Tossing back some frosty glasses of Blue Moon at the same time makes it even better. (Thanks, Darnell.)

So…you got any ideas? Speak up while I grab another pitcher and a few more oranges.

CHAPTER 8

A TECHNOLOGICAL BREAKTHROUGH

Several readers have expressed disappointment over the fact that I don't have any mouthwatering food pictures in my books. They say a cookbook without pictures is like a cake without icing. In fact, one major TV shopping network refused to consider me because my books don't have any photos.

However, I have two good reasons for the lack of pictures in my books. It's cost prohibitive (we'd have to charge a lot more for the books) and, up until now I couldn't afford the technology and equipment to do so. Heck, when I first started writing years and years ago, I did it all on a computer at the library.

But all that has changed. I recently came into some extra cash (the Santa in front of Wal-Mart barely put up a fight when I grabbed his kettle and hightailed it) so I treated myself to an early Christmas present and purchased an iPad on eBay. Okay, it's not technically an iPad. The name at the top says Etch-a-Sketch. The unique name suggests that it's probably an Apple clone manufactured by a company somewhere in Eastern Europe. I'm thinking what used to be Yugoslavia.

The important thing is I finally upgraded my writing gear for half the price of an actual iPad. I mean, why pay top dollar if you can get something close? Am I on this planet just so Apples stock value can surpass another trillion dollars? I think not.

Of course, I'm well aware that my clone may not have all of the features of a real iPad, but d'you know what's really cool? Whenever the screen freezes, all I have to do is turn it upside down and shake it to reboot.

Let's see an iPad do that.

At any rate, for this book I decided to include a few pictures. I think it'll enhance your culinary reading experience, and it just may put me on clear trajectory to win a James Beard Award.

Here's a pic of the fried eggs I made this morning:

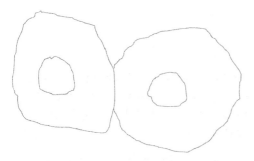

Pretty cool, huh? Now this is me smiling after I ate the eggs:

I think I'm really getting the hang of this! (Did you notice how my eyes resemble the picture of the fried eggs? (That type of continuity is known in the industry as 'branding'). Now, this next picture is.

Oops...crap...

The screen froze up again.

Gotta reboot...

• PERFECT FRIED EGG BREAKFAST •
(With Glazed Canadian Bacon and Old School Home Fries)

PREP: 10 minutes   COOK: 20 minutes

FOR THE EGGS:
INGREDIENTS
  4 large eggs

  2 teaspoons olive or canola oil

  1 tablespoon unsalted butter (cold)

  Kosher salt and fresh cracked pepper to taste

DIRECTIONS
  1. Heat oil in a 12-inch nonstick skillet over low heat for 5 minutes. Meanwhile, crack 2 eggs into a small bowl; crack remaining eggs into second small bowl.

  2. Increase the heat to medium-high until oil shimmers. Add the butter and swirl to coat. Quickly pour two eggs on one side of pan and the other eggs on other side. Season with salt and pepper, cover and cook for 1 minute.

  3. Remove skillet from heat and let sit for 15 – 45 seconds for runny yolks (when checking eggs, just crack the lid to get a peek so all of the steam won't escape), 45 – 60 seconds for medium yolks, and up to 2 minutes for harder yolks.

Slide eggs onto plate and serve.

FOR THE CANADIAN BACON:

INGREDIENTS

1 tablespoon Dijon mustard

1 teaspoon pure maple syrup

Pinch of cayenne pepper to taste (a little goes a long way!)

4 (1/4-inch) slices Canadian bacon

DIRECTIONS

Preheat broiler or toaster oven. Whisk the mustard, syrup and cayenne in a small bowl. Place bacon on a broiler pan or baking sheet and broil 3 inches from the heat for 3 – 4 minutes. Turn and brush with the glaze. Broil for 3 – 4 minutes more or until bacon is well done.

FOR THE POTATOES:

INGREDIENTS

2 russet or large Yukon gold potatoes,

1 small onion, sliced thin

1 tablespoon unsalted butter

2 teaspoons olive or canola oil

1 clove garlic, minced or pressed

1/2 teaspoon paprika

Kosher salt and freshly ground pepper to taste

DIRECTIONS

1.   Nuke the potatoes for 8 minutes (you can do this the night before and put in the fridge). When cool enough to handle, slice into 1/8 to 1/4-inch slices.

2.   Melt butter in a 10-inch skillet over medium-high heat. Add oil.

3.   Add potatoes and cook for 5 minutes. Add the onions and sauté for 5 minutes. Add garlic and sauté for 1 more minute. Season with paprika, salt and pepper.

Toast some bread or English muffins and serve it all with piping hot coffee and a cold glass of OJ.

CHAPTER 9

WHEN A BREAKTHROUGH BECOMES A BUST

The people have spoken. My attempt at posting pics on my blog and in my book was a complete bust. I think *Table for Two* fan Nikki D summed it up best when she wrote to me and said, "Man, Caterson, your pics suck. I'm serious, they really suck. In fact, the last time I saw so much sucking was when I -"

Okay. We'll stop there.

So now I'm back to just writing prose in the hope that your vivid imagination will fill in the blanks.

After all, it works in other areas. Leading experts in the science of human sexuality believe that it's not the genitals, but the mind that is the strongest sex organ. And if what I think about 94% of the time is any indication, I'd have to agree with the experts.

But back to food. I'm afraid I'll have to leave the delectably delicious photos to those who already do it well. For the rest of us? Read with an open and creative mind. Let the pictures unfold in your imagination and smile.

And if you need something a little more concrete and tactile, you can always stop by the house. I always have something cooking and there's always enough.

PS. Anyone need an iPad clone? I got one for sale. Cheap...

• HOMEMADE EGG MUFFINS •

Okay, so you may not have time to whip together an old fashioned breakfast from the previous chapter. If that's the case, here's a recipe for an egg muffin. To really speed things up, purchase a microwave egg cooker at the local big box store. It looks like the plastic things folks put over their eyes when they're at the beach or tanning salon, except bigger. If you like egg muffins, you'll use it often.

PREP: 5 minutes   COOK: 5 minutes

INGREDIENTS
   2 large eggs
   2 English muffins
   2 slices Canadian bacon
   2 slices cheddar cheese
   4 pats butter
   Kosher salt and freshly ground pepper to taste

DIRECTIONS
1.   Crack and place an egg in each compartment of your egg cooker. Cook according to directions.

2.   Toast 2 English muffins.

3.   In the meantime, preheat a small non-stick skillet over medium heat. Add the Canadian bacon and cook, turning once, until heated through and slightly brown. Place a slice of cheese on each slice and cook briefly until cheese begins to melt.

4.   Butter the English muffins and place an egg on the bottom half. Top with Canadian bacon and cheese. Pour a cup of coffee and enjoy!

CHAPTER 10

A NEAR PLETHORA OF INCREDIBLE COOKING TIPS AND KITCHEN HINTS

When I first started posting lists of helpful cooking hints and kitchen tips in my cookbooks, the public responded with a plethora of e-mails, cards and letters demanding "More! More!"

Well, actually, it was more like a stray comment here and there. Something more akin to: "What? Is that it?" or "Is that all you got?"

My answer? A resounding NO! Here are a few more. Now keep those cards and letters coming!

Concerning Those Who Use the Word 'Plethora'
You can pretty much discount the credibility of anyone who uses the word 'plethora' in any form of written or oral communication. If they use it twice in the same communication, feel free to hunt them down and beat them with a thesaurus.

Microwave Ovens - The Miracle Appliance that Wasn't
When microwave ovens were first introduced they were supposed to revolutionize our culinary lives. Manufacturers claimed that these modern marvels would do everything except crush garlic and wash dishes. I've owned a microwave for over three decades and have found that it excels at only four things: popping bags of popcorn, defrosting or cooking frozen veggies, reheating last night's dinner, and taking up two square feet of precious counter space. Reports that it can also dry wet cats are purely speculative.

When Dinner Guests Show Up Early
Many of us make a real effort to show up for a dinner party a little late. This is good form. However, there's a very small minority who insist on showing up early. Sometimes very early. When these socially-inept morons show up while you're finishing a sauce or fluffing the rice, throw some sliced onions in a skillet with some olive oil and sauté them. Trust me, the aroma will drive 'em nuts but they won't be able to eat anything. (Oh, and be sure you pour some of cheap 'cooking wine' in a carafe and set it out. Save the real stuff for those guests who know how to show up at the right time).

Keeping Your Fridge Smelling Fresh

Placing an open box of baking soda in the back of the fridge to keep it odor-free is a strategy that has been handed down from great-grandparents to grandparents and parents. Unfortunately, it doesn't really work. Here's the best way to keep your fridge odor-free: Make sure all of your food is tightly wrapped and keep the refrigerator clean. I know it's more work than putting a little yellow box on the shelf, but this technique actually works.

Skinning Chicken

Removing chicken skin with your bare hands works just fine with the first piece. After that your fingers get so slimy you may as well have had them dipped in oil. Instead, use a paper towel to grasp the skin and then toss the paper towel when you're done. No muss. No fuss.

Quick Thawing Steaks and Chops

The quickest way to thaw frozen steaks and chops is to place them in a heavy aluminum skillet or baking pan (the heavier and thicker, the better) at room temperature. You'll be amazed at how quickly they defrost. Of course, thicker roasts and chicken should only be defrosted in the fridge.

Quick Thawing Fish Steaks

Most frozen fish is flash-frozen and vacuum wrapped. Just place the wrapped fish in a bowl of water and they'll thaw out in a flash.

Quick Thawing Shrimp

Place frozen shrimp in a colander and run them under warm water.

Cooking Fresh Spinach

A pound of fresh spinach looks like it could feed a small army, but when it cooks down it only yields about one cup. Keep that in mind when you're out shopping.

Late Night Gadget Infomercials

The effectiveness of any gadget advertised on a late night infomercial is diminished in proportion to the amount of airtime said infomercial expends.

CHAPTER 11

DON'T YOU GO AND GIVE ME ANY SAUCE, 'CUZ CHILD, I GOT SAUCE THAT'S OLDER THAN YOU

Some things improve with age. I'm thinking about things like scotch, blue jeans, baseball mitts, and most wines.

Some things do not. Like bread, lettuce, Silly Putty, or my ability to impress beautiful women.

But there's one item that definitely will improve with age: Chinese Looing Sauce.

This sauce was created over 2000 years ago and is used to braise a wide variety of meats. Technically, this is called a Master Sauce but in some culinary corners it's referred to as a Loo Shui Sauce. I prefer to call it Looed Sauce. Mainly because it sounds so weird.

You can use this sauce to braise chicken (see below), pork, beef, duck or lamb (but never seafood).

And the best part? The more you use it, the better it gets.

Just be sure to skim the fat and re-fresh the ingredients every now and then. After each use, freeze, and then bring to a boil before using again. Some Master Sauces in China are over 100 years old and are passed down from generation to generation.

Below I've included a recipe for "Chicken in Master Sauce". Of course, when I serve it to guests I prefer to call it by its other name: "Looed Chicken". I always love to see the look on their faces.

Chicken will take under 30 minutes to cook. Beef, pork and lamb I cut into serving portions. They should take 30 - 40 minutes. Be sure to check the temperature with a meat thermometer.

Oh, and for the record, my looing sauce is over 30 years old (yet another point I mention to get a rise out of my guests). I plan to pass it down to my grandkids someday.

• CHINESE LOOING SAUCE •

PREP: 5 minutes   COOK: 25 minutes

INGREDIENTS
  2 cups beef broth
  2 cups chicken broth
  2 cups soy sauce
  1/2 cup rice wine or dry sherry
  5 slices peeled fresh ginger
  2 cloves garlic, peeled
  2 tablespoons brown sugar
  2 whole star anise pods (Badia® is a common brand. It's usually found with the spices in the ethnic or international aisle of most grocery stores)
  1 stick cinnamon
  5 black peppercorns

DIRECTIONS
  Bring all the ingredients to a boil in dutch oven over high heat. Add the wings and reduce heat to low. Simmer for about 20 minutes.

• LOOED CHICKEN WINGS •

Prep: 5 minutes   Cook: 25 minutes

INGREDIENTS
  Looing Sauce
  16 chicken wing pieces (no tips) or 4 chicken thighs

DIRECTIONS
  Bring Looing Sauce to a boil in a dutch oven or other pot over high heat. Add chicken and return to a boil. Turn heat to low and simmer for 20 - 25 minutes until chicken is done. Remove and serve hot or at room temperature.

CHAPTER 12

I CHEAT AND SO CAN YOU

Before you get all excited, I'm not talking about cheating on your fiancé, spouse or the IRS.

I'm talking about cheating in the kitchen.

Cuz let's face it, most of us don't have the extra cash or time to seek out exotic or hard-to-find ingredients like baby zucchini, hubbard squash, quince, daikon, or blueberry bush wood chips (for grilling), all of which I've come across in some of my cooking mag recipes.

And I'm sure most of us don't have the time to create everything from scratch in the kitchen.

So Chef Warren says it's okay to cheat a little.

But it's just not me. I learned to cheat from reading books by cooking icons Pierre Franey, James Beard, Julee Rosso & Sheila Lukins (of Silver Palate Cookbook fame) and yes, even the unforgettable Jacques Pepin.

If these luminaries can cheat, so can the likes of you and I.

First things first. If I come across a recipe that calls for something I can't pick up at my local grocery store or farmer's market. I don't make it. There's so many recipes using fresh and readily available ingredients to choose from that I see no need to run all over town looking for something that I'll probably only use once.

As far as the cheating thing? There was a time in my life when I was feeding 7 or more people every night. So it made sense for me to make a big pot o' beans or beef broth from scratch. I also had lots of freezer space so it was practical to make beans, broths, tomato sauce, and other items from scratch to store in one of my chest freezers.

Since I'm no longer cooking for that many people and my chest freezers found their way to Craig's List, I've learned how to 'cheat' from some of my literary mentors. Here are just some of the things I keep on hand in my freezer or cupboard:

Canned Tomatoes – I use canned tomatoes for almost all cooking applications. I buy both whole and chopped (I particularly like Hunt's®, especially their fire-roasted chopped tomatoes). Aside from being convenient, I find that canned tomatoes are often more flavorful than fresh.

Canned Beans – I know I can make beans a lot cheaper from scratch, but as I mentioned above, I don't have a lot of freezer space to store a bunch of plastic containers full of beans. Plus, I like the convenience of having to simply open a can or two if I have a hankering for a hearty soup, stew or chili.

Frozen Veggies – I have a wonderful grocery store near me called Detwiler's that has some of the best fresh produce I've ever seen at unbelievable prices. Since it's just down the street I probably use more fresh veggies than the average person. That being said, I don't have a problem with frozen veggies like corn, peas, string beans, lima beans, spinach and mixed veggies. I buy them plain, not the sauced up varieties. Veggies like asparagus, broccoli, cauliflower, or carrots I try to buy fresh because they're crisper after cooking than their frozen bretheren. But I've been known to stock these as well if I'm not looking for the 'crispness' factor.

Soup Base – There was a time when I would make a big batch of broth from scratch. But since I no longer have the storage space to freeze bones or finished broth, I use what's known as a soup base. This is a paste that comes in many flavors: beef, chicken, ham, vegetable, mushroom, shrimp, lobster, clam, etc. The nice thing about a true soup base is that, unlike bouillon cubes, the first, and main, ingredient is not salt. So if you buy a beef base, the first ingredient is going to be beef. Chicken? Chicken. Lobster? Lobster. You use 1 teaspoon of base for each cup of water. Even the smaller jars will make 38 cups (for about $4 a jar). That's much more frugal than boxed or canned broths. Better than Bouillon®, Tone's®, and Minor's® are all great brands.

Frozen Hashed Brown Potatoes – Again, I love potatoes made from scratch, but if I'm pressed for time and want to add some potatoes to my soup or stew, I just toss in some frozen potatoes and move forward.

Ramen Noodles – Sure, many of us lived off this super-convenient and cheap food product in college or grad school, but I still keep a stash in my cupboard for those nights when I want a lightning quick meal that's open to all kinds of interpretation (see Chapter 15). Just make sure you toss the silver packet in the trash and pull out your soup base to make it.

Frozen Fruit – As I mentioned above, I'm fortunate to have a great market around the corner. But sometimes the fruit I want isn't in season; so I buy frozen fruit to use in desserts, ice pops, soups, etc.

Bread Crumbs – What's so hard about throwing some day old bread in the food processor or blender? Nothing. My problem is freezer space. So I keep both panko and regular bread crumbs in my pantry for emergencies.

Pasta Sauce – This is another item that you can make from scratch. For me, again, it's storage. So I keep a couple of jars on hand. I buy them when they're bogo. Find a brand you like and do the same.

Salad Dressings - I still make Italian Dressing or Balsamic Vinaigrette from scratch because I can do so in about the same amount of time it takes me to open a bottle. Plus, I can make it in whatever amount I need that night. But when it comes to blue cheese, ranch, Russian or other less-than-easy to prepare dressings, I opt for bottled. Find a brand you like and get them on sale.

CHAPTER 13

ST. PADDY'S DAY AND IRISH CUISINE – IT'S NOT AN OXYMORON

"It's been said that God created whiskey to keep the Irish from taking over the world. If so, then He also created haggis to keep the Scots from going into the restaurant business." ~ Chef Warren

I sometimes write restaurant reviews for Yelp, Zamato, and TripAdvisor when an establishment warrants my two cents worth.

Or if I have way too much time on my hands.

On a recent evening when I had so much time on my hands I had to use a Brillo Pad to get it all off, I decided to write a review for one of my favorite Irish pubs. But before doing so, I scanned some reviews for this particular pub as well as some others just to see what folks were saying. I was amazed that several reviewers of Irish pubs had the néatóg to complain about the cuisine.

Listen. Going to an Irish pub for "the cuisine" is like going to Mardi Gras because you want to stock up on some great jewelry.

Nope, folks go to Irish pubs for the great atmosphere, the great company (even a stranger is welcomed), the great beer, and the great music. The food? If it's not moving and it's warm, you'll find it adequate and it'll surely stick to your ribs. If it were served in any other setting it would probably be forgettable.

But make no mistake, when the waitress sets that bowl of Irish stew on your table, and the Guinness begins to flow, and the fellah with the guitar up front explains the 'origin of this next song', and the whole room bursts into a rousing rendition of 'Whiskey in a Jar'...well, then you know you've entered another realm where the work-a-day world falls to the floor like tattered rags and joy reigns triumphant. This is especially true on St. Patrick's Day.

Most of the dishes you'll find on the menu in your average Irish pub in America are more Irish-American than they are Irish. Here's a few Irish-American dishes to add to your repertoire.

Now let's all pour a pint and be thankful that Scottish eating establishments are few and far between.

• AN IRISH-AMERICAN FEAST •
CORNED BEEF, COLCANNON AND SODA-BREAD

Interestingly, corned beef (or corned beef and cabbage) is rarely eaten in Ireland. Historically, the Irish did breed cattle but kept them mainly as work animals and for milk. Beef was somewhat of luxury and still is. What the Irish consider their 'national dish' is boiled bacon and cabbage. Now when the Irish speak of bacon, they're not referring to what we call bacon; the smoked strips from the pig's belly. No, when they speak of bacon they mean any part of the pig except for the rear leg, or ham. Very similar to how we refer to most pig meat as pork. Corned beef became popular here in the states when the first waves of immigrants arrived because beef was cheaper than pork. It's especially popular around St. Paddy's Day. But it's so good; feel free to serve this meal year round! This will feed 6 - 8 people.

• TRADITIONAL CORNED BEEF AND CABBAGE •

PREP: 10 minutes   COOK: 1-1/2 hours

INGREDIENTS
   3 or 4 pounds corned beef brisket with spice packet
   10 small red potatoes (cut them in half if large)
   5 carrots, peeled and cut into 3-inch pieces
   1 large head cabbage, cut into small wedges

DIRECTIONS
1. Place corned beef in large pot or Dutch oven and cover with water. Add the spice packet that came with the corned beef. Cover pot and bring to a boil, then reduce to a simmer. Simmer approximately 50 minutes per pound or until tender.

2. Add whole potatoes and carrots, and cook until the vegetables are almost tender. Add cabbage and cook for 15 more minutes. Remove meat and let rest 15 minutes.

3. Place vegetables in a bowl and cover. Add as much broth (cooking liquid reserved in the Dutch oven or large pot) as you want. Slice meat across the grain. Serve along with vegetables.

• COOKING OUTSIDE THE LINES CORNED BEEF •

The oranges and prunes give this version a bit of a somewhat non-Irish twist. But that's okay. We are cooking outside the lines, aren't we? And instead of cooking the cabbage with the corned beef, we're going to cook them with the taters. It's a traditional dish called colcannon.

FOR THE CORNED BEEF:

PREP: 10 minutes

SOAK: 1 hour

COOK: 4+ hours

INGREDIENTS

3 or 4 pounds corned beef brisket

2 cups baby carrots

1 cup diced celery

1/2 cup slice onions

1/2 cup prunes

1 orange, sliced

1 bay leaf

3 tablespoons brown sugar

1 tablespoon orange juice

DIRECTIONS
1. Place corned beef in a dutch oven or other large pot and cover with water. Soak for 1 hour. Rinse and pat dry.

2. Preheat oven to 350°. Place a piece of heavy-duty tin foil cut large enough to wrap the corned beef in a baking or roasting pan. Add the corned beef and place the carrots, celery, onions, prunes, orange slices, and the bay leaf on top. Seal the brisket and bake for 3-1/2 hours.

3. Towards the end, combine the orange juice and brown sugar in a small pan over medium-high heat. Stir to dissolve. Open the foil and baste the brisket with the orange glaze. Bake uncovered for 30 more minutes.

4. Remove and let stand for 15 minutes before slicing.

FOR THE COLCANNON:

PREP: 15 minutes   COOK: 20 minutes

INGREDIENTS

    2 pounds russet or Yukon gold potatoes, peeled and cubed

    5 slices bacon, chopped

    1/2 small head of cabbage, chopped (about 5 cups)

    1 medium onion chopped

    3/4 cup milk

    Kosher salt and freshly ground pepper to taste

    4 tablespoons unsalted butter, melted

DIRECTIONS

1. Place potatoes in a medium-sized saucepan with enough water to cover. Bring to a boil, lower heat to medium-low and simmer until the potatoes are tender, about 15 minutes.

2. Meanwhile, place the bacon in a 10-inch skillet over medium-high heat and sauté until evenly browned. Remove the bacon with a slotted spoon and set aside. Add the cabbage and onions to the drippings and sauté until the onions are soft and translucent, about 10 minutes.

3. Drain the potatoes and return to the saucepan. Shake to remove excess moisture. Add the milk and mash the potatoes. Season with kosher salt and freshly ground pepper to taste. Add the bacon, cabbage and onion and stir until well mixed.

4. Transfer the Colcannon to a medium sized bowl and drizzle the melted butter over the top. Serve immediately.

CHAPTER 14

TEN IRISH FACTS, WHISKEY CHICKEN, AND WHY THE WORLD WILL NEVER RUN OUT OF GUINNESS

While we're still celebrating St. Patrick's Day, I thought I'd offer these valuable Irish facts and some traditional Irish recipes. Now let's raise a glass and toast our forefathers and mothers - those saints and sinners who brought so much inspiration and laughter to our lives. And even if you don't have a drop of Irish blood in you, we are all Irish every March 17th. *Slainte'!*

Ten Irish facts we all would do well to remember:

1. Legend has it that St. Brendan discovered America 1,000 years before Columbus. Legend also has it that when he arrived at 10 am and saw that the pubs weren't open yet, he turned ship and headed back to Ireland.

2. The Seven Celtic Nations are: Ireland, Scotland, Wales, Isle of Man, Cornwall, Brittany, and Galicia. For nearly 100 years South Boston has petitioned to be included, but that would've meant re-printing all the Seven Celtic Nations t-shirts, posters, flags and other stuff, so it never really gained traction.

3. The phrase "tying the knot" originated in Ireland and referred to the ancient marriage custom of "handfasting". It had nothing to do with what randy newlyweds do when presented with a four-poster bed and a handful of neckties.

4. Just a few years ago there were more Polish folks in Ireland than there were native Irish. That this occurred because Ireland had a surplus of vowels and was running low on consonants is purely speculative.

5. One of the largest and most famous festivals in the world starts on March 17th, when over 500,000 people line the streets of Dublin to watch the St. Paddy's Day Parade. Then they will flood the local pubs to carry on the celebration, which continues uninterrupted until March 16th of the following year.

6. There are over 36 million United States residents with Irish ancestry. That's nearly 12% of the population. However, on St. Paddy's Day, those who claim Irish ancestry make up 127% of the population.

7. Ireland's top star in the sport of hurling is Sean Og O'Hailpin who plays for the County Cork Team. America's top star in hurling is Danny "The Whale" O'Shannon from Chicago. You can catch Danny in action every Friday night down at Schaller's Pump. For the best hurling, wait until after 11 pm when he has already downed a couple of pints of Smithwick's and a few burgers. Just be sure to watch your step when old Danny stops hurling.

8. The Irish Academy of Engineers recommends that an under-sea tunnel be built to link Ireland and Wales. They envision trains running at speeds of 150 mph between Rosslare, Ireland and Fishguard, Wales. Currently, there's no financial backer for such a project mainly because they have yet to figure out why anyone from Ireland would want to visit Wales.

9. The tallest identical twins ever born (7ft 2in) were the Brothers Knipe from Magherafelt, County Derry in 1761. However, due to their size, one Knipe brother was born in March while the other was born sometime in late April.

10. Why the world will never run out of Guinness: the original Guinness Brewery in Dublin has a 9,000 year lease on its property and they pay an annual rate of 45 Irish pounds a year, which is about 75 bucks in US dollars.

• SMOKED SAUSAGE AND CABBAGE •

While boiled bacon and cabbage is the national dish, sometimes there's not enough time to throw that meal together. Here's a traditional Irish dish that has a similar flavor and texture in a fraction of the time. This will serve 2 but it's easy to double.

PREP: 10 minutes   COOK: 20 minutes

INGREDIENTS
    1/2 pound smoked sausage or kielbasa, cut into 2-inch pieces

    1 tablespoon olive or canola oil

    3 cups coarsely chopped cabbage

    1 small onion, cut into small wedges

    1 clove garlic, minced or pressed

    1/4 teaspoon sugar (or a bit more to taste)

    1/8 teaspoon caraway seeds

    Kosher salt and freshly ground pepper to taste

DIRECTIONS
    1.   Heat a 10-inch skillet over medium-high heat. Add the oil and swirl to coat.
          Add the sausage and sauté until lightly brown and heated through, about 3 –
          5 minutes. Transfer to a plate and cover to keep warm.

    2.   Add the cabbage, onion, garlic sugar, caraway seeds, salt and pepper.
          Sauté until the onions begin to brown a little, about 5 minutes. Return the
          sausage to the skillet, cover and cook for 3 minutes. Remove skillet from
          heat and let stand for 5 minutes to allow the flavors to meld.

• DUBLIN LAWYER •

This dish is very rich. Perhaps that's why they named it Dublin Lawyer - 'cuz only a lawyer could afford it! As a result, you certainly wouldn't want to eat it every night. Or every week for that matter. It's traditionally made with the meat from a 2-pound lobster, but we're being frugal so we're substituting extra-large shrimp. If you can find Argentinean Red Shrimp, go for it - the flavor is a lot like lobster. I like to serve this in shallow bowls with just a salad and lots of bread to soak up the sauce. Serves 2.

PREP: Less than 5 minutes   COOK: 5 minutes

INGREDIENTS

3/4 pound extra-large shrimp, peeled and deveined

1/3 cup Kerry Gold butter, cut into pats

1/3 cup Jameson's Irish Whiskey

1/3 cup heavy cream

Kosher salt and freshly ground pepper to taste

Chopped fresh parsley or chives to garnish

DIRECTIONS

Melt butter over medium heat in a 10-inch skillet. Add shrimp and sauté until almost done, about 2 - 3 minutes. Add the whiskey and, after a moment when it's heated, touch a lit kitchen match to the edge of the skillet to flambé (watch your face!). When the flame dies out, add the cream and let it bubble and heat. Season with salt and pepper, then garnish with chopped parsley.

• JAMESON WHISKEY STUFFED STEAK •

This traditional steak dish is a riff on steak diane – with a nice twist: you stuff the steak before grilling it.

PREP: 5 minutes   COOK: 25 minutes

INGREDIENTS
2 (6 – 8 ounce) boneless ribeye steaks at least 1-inch thick, butterflied

1/2 cup unsalted butter (Kerrygold for authenticity), divided

1 cup fresh bread crumbs (or substitute plain Panko bread crumbs)

Pinch of thyme

Kosher salt and fresh ground pepper to taste

2 tablespoons Jameson Irish Whiskey

2 tablespoons olive or canola oil

1 large shallot (or one medium onion) diced, about 1/2 cup

6 baby portobello mushrooms, sliced

DIRECTIONS
1. Heat a small skillet over medium heat and add 2 tablespoons butter. When the butter melts, swirl to coat and add the bread crumbs, thyme, salt and pepper. Cook until bread crumbs have absorbed the butter, about 2 minutes. Stir in the whiskey then spread half the mixture in the center of each steak. Close the steaks and press shut with the palm of your hand.

2. Heat a 10-inch skillet over medium-high heat. Add the oil and when it just begins to shimmer, add the steaks. Cook until seared on one side, about 3 minutes. Turn and sear on the other side, about 3 additional minutes. Transfer steaks to a plate and cover.

3. Turn the heat to medium and add the remaining butter to melt. Stir in the shallots and mushroom and sauté until tender, about 5 – 8 minutes. Move the vegetables to the perimeter return the steaks to center of the skillet. Continue to cook, turning often, until steaks are done to your liking, about 6 – 8 minutes for medium-rare.

4. Place the steaks in the center of 2 plates and spoon the mushroom mixture and pan juices over each one.

• JAMESON WHISKEY CHICKEN •

Since we have the whiskey out, let's use some in this delicious pub dish. It's very similar to Dublin Lawyer, but is a lot cheaper to prepare.

PREP: 5 minutes   COOK: 45 minutes

INGREDIENTS
   2 chicken leg quarters
   2 tablespoons unsalted butter, softened
   Kosher salt and freshly ground pepper to taste
   Juice of half a lemon (about 1-1/2 tablespoons)
   2 tablespoons Jameson or other Irish whiskey
   1/3 cup heavy cream

DIRECTIONS
1.   Preheat oven to 400°.

2.   Place the chicken in a cast iron skillet (or a roasting pan that can sit on the stove). Rub the chicken all over (and under the skin) with butter. Season with salt and pepper to taste then drizzle the lemon juice over each piece.

3.   Put the cast iron skillet into the oven and roast until an instant read thermometer registers 165°, about 35 – 40 minutes. Transfer chicken to a plate and cover to keep warm.

4.   Pour or spoon off fat from the skillet and set the pan over medium heat on the stove. Pour the whiskey into the pan and let it heat for a moment. Step back and set a match to the edge of the skillet to let the whiskey flambé. When the flame dies out, add the cream and stir to scrape up any brown bits on the bottom. Spoon the sauce over the chicken and serve.

• CHAMP •
(Irish Mashed Potatoes)

PREP: 10 minutes   COOK: 20 minutes

INGREDIENTS

2 large russet or other baking potatoes, peeled and quartered

1/4 cup, plus 2 tablespoons half and half (or milk for a lighter dish)

2 tablespoons unsalted butter, plus a couple of pats for serving (Kerrygold for authenticity)

3 tablespoons sliced chives or green scallion tops

Kosher salt and fresh ground pepper to taste

DIRECTIONS

1. Place the potatoes in a large saucepan and add cold water to cover. Bring to a boil over medium-high heat and add a pinch of salt. Reduce heat to medium and simmer until potatoes are tender, about 12 – 15 minutes. Drain well and return potatoes to the saucepan. Shake the pan for a few moments to dry them out a bit.

2. Meanwhile, heat the half and half in a saucepan over medium heat. Add the chives or scallions and cook until just heated through.

3. Mash the potatoes along with the butter. Slowly add the half and half mixture, stirring with a fork or spoon, until fluffy. Season with salt and pepper to taste.

4. Spoon a half the potatoes on each plate and make a small dent in the top. Place a pat of butter in each one and serve.

• BOILED CARROTS •

Carrots are traditionally prepared in the same water in which bacon (pork) or corned beef had been boiled. However, they make a mighty fine dish when simply boiled with a tad of sugar and butter. But note, when I say 'boiled' I'm not talking about using a potful of water. This method of preparation is actually closer to steaming than boiling. And that's a good thing because you'll retain more vitamins and minerals that way.

PREP: 5 minutes   COOK: 8 minutes

INGREDIENTS
  1/2 pound carrots, peeled (if desired) and slice into 1/4-inch pieces
  1/4 cup water
  1 tablespoon unsalted butter (Kerrygold for authenticity)
  1 tablespoon brown (or white) sugar
  Chopped parsley to garnish

DIRECTIONS
  1. Bring the water and carrots to a boil in 10-inch skillet or large saucepan over medium-high heat. Cover and reduce heat to medium and simmer until carrots are almost tender when poked with a fork (you don't want them mushy) about 3 – 5 minutes.

  2. Uncover and turn heat to high. Cook carrots, stirring often, until the water is almost evaporated, about 1 – 2 minutes. Stir in the butter and sugar. Toss and stir until the carrots are nicely glazed, about 2 – 3 minutes. Sprinkle with parsley to garnish.

CHAPTER 15

IF WE WANT TO EAT DIRT-CHEAP AND LIGHTNING-QUICK, WE BETTER USE OUR NOODLES... RAMEN NOODLES THAT IS

You're hungry. You don't have time to cook and you're strapped for cash. So dining at The French Laundry is out of the question.

Do you have to settle for some kind of meal-deal handed to you through a drive-thru window by a bored and distracted teenager?

No way!

That's why the Good Lord gave us Instant Ramen Noodles.

Well, not directly like He did that manna thing back in the book of Exodus. With ramen noodles He used an intermediary by the name of Momofuku Ando, founder of Nissin Food Corporation. True, Momofuku didn't invent ramen noodles; someone in China's distant past would need to take the credit for that. The dish found it's way to Japan via Chinese tradesmen in the 19th century. It was enthusiastically embraced and became a significant part of the Japanese culinary world. Mr. Ando created an instant version of it after World War II and it took the world by storm.

Heck, Chef David Chang created a restaurant empire serving up $15 bowls of ramen at his celebrated Momofuku restaurants. And although Chef Chang creates his noodles from scratch, you and I can partake of this culinary treasure by virtue of Mr. Ando's ingenuity.

After all, tens of thousands of college students can't be wrong.

And face it. Ramen Noodles are cheap. Stock up and you won't be at a loss when the cash flow is slow or you don't have a lot of time to prepare lunch or dinner. Just don't make them according to the directions on the packet.

I'm going to show you how to take that cheap and lowly packet of dried noodles and turn them into a dish that just might be good enough for company.

But first things first.

When you're at the store picking up a case of ramen noodles, swing by the soup aisle and pick up a jar or two of what's known as soup base. You'll find these by the bouillon cubes.

Essentially, soup base is a paste that you stir into hot water to create a broth. It's what most restaurants use when they cook soup or stews 'from scratch'. The ratio is usually 1 teaspoon of soup base to 1 cup of water.

Most of the jars you buy in the grocery store will make 38 cups for around $4.00 – which is much cheaper than buying soup broth in a can or box. I always have a jar of chicken, beef and vegetable soup base in my fridge. They'll keep for 18 months.

Now that you have some packages of ramen noodles and soup base, let's start with the basics.

• BASIC RAMEN NOODLES •

The first thing I want you to do after you open you bag of ramen is take the silver 'flavor packet' and hurl it in the trash. Trust me, there's nothing in that little packet that's worth eating. (And now that you have some soup base in your fridge, you won't be needing it anyway).

DIRECTIONS
Bring two cups of water to a boil and stir in two teaspoons of soup base until it dissolves. Add your noodles and cook according to the directions. Ladle into bowls and enjoy. That's it.

But why eat plain ramen noodles when you can take it up a notch or two with the addition of a handful of ingredients? Not me. So grab another ramen noodle package and soup base, 'cuz we're gonna cook Momofuku-style starting with:

• DELUXE RAMEN NOODLES •

This is where we get creative. Prepare basic ramen noodles as above then add one, or any combination, of these:

1/4 cup (more depending on how hearty you want the soup) of:

Frozen peas

Frozen carrots

Frozen peas and carrots

Frozen broccoli or cauliflower (diced)

Frozen mixed veggies

Sliced or coarsely chopped mushrooms

Sliced or coarsely chopped leftover cooked chicken, beef or pork

Mixed can of Chinese veggies

Diced leftover veggies (squash, zucchini, onions, carrots, etc)

Leftover chicken, beef or pork, chopped or sliced

Do you see the potential? Check your fridge and cupboard. I'm sure there are more items you can add.

Now that you've taken basic ramen noodles up a notch. Let's take it up yet another notch with these uber-cool recipes. Remember, we're trying to create great soups in a matter of minutes. I have lots of recipes for ramen that require several steps and numerous ingredients (some of them only available in Oriental food stores) but that's not what this chapter is about. We want great noodles in no time with very little fuss. (If you want some recipes for traditional Hot and Sour Soup or Pad Thai shoot me an email. I promise I'll get back to you. For now, let's whip up some bowls of these favorites).

• EASIEST HOT AND SOUR SOUP •

INGREDIENTS
   1 Ramen noodle package

   2 cups water

   2 teaspoons soup base

   1 teaspoon rice vinegar (or white wine vinegar)

   1/8 teaspoon hot sauce (I recommend Sriracha®) or more to taste

   Chopped fresh or dried parsley to garnish (optional)

DIRECTIONS
   1.   Prepare Basic Ramen Noodles as above.

   2.   Stir in vinegar and hot sauce.

   3.   Sprinkle with parsley.

• DELUXE HOT AND SOUR SOUP •

Prepare Basic Hot and Sour Soup as above. Stir in 1/4 cup thinly sliced mushrooms, one beaten egg, and 1 thinly sliced green onion. For a more substantial meal, stir in 2 – 3 tablespoons sliced or chopped leftover cooked meat (chicken, beef, pork, etc).

• COCONUT RAMEN NOODLES •

Prepare Basic Ramen Noodles as above. Then stir in 1/2 cup canned coconut milk. Want to add a little pizzazz? Give it a couple of shots of Sriracha to taste.

• COCONUT CURRY RAMEN NOODLES •

Prepare Coconut Ramen Noodles as above. Stir in 1 tablespoon curry powder (or more or less according to taste) and 1/2 teaspoon Sriracha sauce or 1/4 teaspoon cayenne pepper, or more according to taste.

• EGGS-TRAORDINARY RAMEN NOODLES •

Prepare Basic Ramen Noodles as above. Ladle into two bowls and top each bowl with a hard-boiled, soft-boiled, poached, or fried egg.

• PAD THAI STYLE RAMEN NOODLES •

1.   Prepare Basic Ramen Noodles as above.

2.   Stir in 2 tablespoons peanut butter and 1/8 teaspoon Sriracha sauce

• PENNSYLVANIA CORN CHOWDER RAMEN NOODLES •

1. Prepare Basic Ramen Noodles as above.

2. Stir in 1/4 cup frozen or canned corn

3. Ladle into 2 bowls and top each with a pat of butter.

• RAMEN NOODLES ALFREDO •

1. Prepare Basic Ramen Noodles as above.

2. Reserve 1/3 cup broth and drain noodles.

3. Add 2 tablespoons unsalted butter to the saucepan. When melted,add 1 clove minced or pressed garlic and sauté until fragrant, about 1 minute. Return the ramen noodles to the saucepan and toss. Stir in 1/3 cup grated Parmesan cheese (not jarred) then stir in the reserved broth. Garnish with 2 teaspoons parsley.

CHAPTER 16

FIVE KITCHEN DISASTERS AND FIVE EASY FIXES

I know I promised some kitchen tips for meals gone wrong in a previous chapter, but I was distracted by St. Paddy's Day, so I had to give my two cents' worth on Irish cuisine. I even wrote about Irish cuisine on an international food website. Many enjoyed the post, but it also raised some hackles.

It appears some folks were offended that I would dare address the shortcomings of Irish cuisine (I did dare), some asked if I'd ever really been to Ireland (no, but it's on my bucket list), and one went ballistic over my use of Irish stereotypes -- drinking, dancing, etc. (as if *that's* never been done before).

Well, to all those whose sense of humor has gone down the drain like a pint of flat Guinness I have this to say: *Póg mo thóin* (which as many of you already know is Irish for 'thanks for your suggestions').

Now that I got that out of the way, let's move on.

In another chapter I said if it ain't broke don't fix it. Some recipes are perfect just the way they are. Some could use some tweaking to make them better (hence the concept of this book). And some are just so down right awful that there's no use trying to rescue them. They just can't be fixed.

Just like disasters in other parts of our lives.

For instance:

When I was a freshman in college our school hosted weekend events to attract new students. At one such event, I was seated next to a gorgeous high school senior during dinner. How gorgeous? My goodness, her skin was radiant, her blonde hair gave the sun a run for its money, and her eyes danced like an Irish maid after two shots of Jameson's.

I was smitten.

During the course of our conversation and laughter, she asked me if I knew the head of our choral music department. In my rush to be witty and oh-so-impressive I replied, "You mean Old Leather Lungs?" (The student body's pet name for her.)

Her dancing eyes turned dark and her face folded up in a sneer.

"That's my grandmother," she spat.

I couldn't fix that.

Didn't even try.

So as in life, sometimes a dish turns out so bad it's impossible to fix. But here are some kitchen disasters that you can rectify. Like these:

SOUP, STEW, OR GRAVY THAT'S TOO SALTY

I've seen more than my share of books and websites suggesting that you put some sliced potatoes into the dish and continue to cook it so the potatoes absorb the salt. Then you have to simply remove the salt-soaked potato and move forward. Sorry, but that simply won't work. Imagine putting a sponge or two in a bucket of very salty water. When you remove the sponge do you think the water will be any less salty? Nope. That's because you're removing water along with the salt. Bottom line? The only way to reduce the saltiness of a sauce or soup is to dilute it by adding more broth or other liquid.

OVERCOOKED, DRIED-OUT MEAT

We've all made steak, chops or chicken breasts that were overcooked and dry. How can we remedy it so our dinner guests don't spend the rest of the evening gnawing and gnashing on tough-as-leather meat? Here's one ploy I've used with great success: Pour any drippings into a saucepan, add (depending on how much meat you've made) one to four cups of beef or chicken stock and a tablespoon or two of wine, and bring to a boil. Slice the meat, place it in a roasting pan or casserole dish, and pour the stock mixture over it. Cover with foil and place it in a warm oven for five minutes. The meat will not only be edible, but also will actually taste good. And it beats feeding it all to the dog.

BURNED SOUP OR STEW

How many of us have labored over a great soup or stew only to have it burn when our backs are turned? I had a friend who had a knack for creating a delicious Caribbean stew. After setting it on the stove to simmer one Sunday afternoon, he decided it was a good time to down a couple of jumbo margaritas to while away the time. I heard he woke up late sometime on Monday. The whole thing had to be ditched because it appeared the stew and the metal of the pan fused to create a new alloy.

However, if you limit your margarita imbibing and catch your stew before it has a chance to burn too much, don't stir it. Instead, gently ladle the stew into a new pot. Be sure you start ladling from the top, tasting each ladleful until it starts to taste burnt. At that point you can ditch the rest.

SAUCE, DRESSING OR SOUP THAT'S TOO HOT OR SPICY

Not everyone shares my proclivity for spicy foods and at times I even go overboard. So how can you tame the heat once it's lit? You can lower the temp a bit by adding a touch of sweetness via a few diced tomatoes (good) or a squirt or two of ketchup (better). Adding diced sweet fruit (mangoes, peaches, etc.) or fruit juice will help as well. You can also turn it down a notch by adding a glop or two of plain yogurt (pretty effective in curries), cream, or even milk. And if you have the time and ingredients, you might want to create another batch without the hot stuff, then combine the two. That would cut your heat in half.

LUMPY GRAVY

I like my potatoes smashed as opposed to whipped because I like to bite into bits of potatoes in my mashed potatoes. However, I don't like to bite into chunks of flour in my gravy. Your guests probably don't either. Here's a remedy for that: Pour the gravy into a blender (but not more than halfway or you'll have a mess on your hands) and process until the gravy is smooth. This should take around 30 seconds or so. Then pour the gravy through a wire-mesh strainer into another pan and reheat.

OVERCOOKED VEGGIES

With the exception of many all-you-can-eat buffet cooks, no one really likes to serve up mushy vegetables. Here's a quick (and cute) way to redeem vegetables that have been tortured into submission: Melt a tablespoon of butter in a small saucepan then add 1 tablespoon flour. Cook and stir for a few minutes until smooth. Slowly add 1/3-cup milk and stir over medium-low heat until thickened. Add 2 cups of the wilted veggies then sprinkle with salt, pepper, and/or a pinch of herb of choice. Heat through and voilá - creamed veggies! (Or as I like to call them: *Légumes à la Crème.*)

Now if you'll excuse me, I think I smell something burning. Hold my margarita, will ya?

CHAPTER 17

WHEN DR. FRANKENSTEIN COOKS FOR IGOR

Have you ever sat down to a tantalizing meal of whitefish, sodium benzoate, cracker crumbs, partially hydrogenated cottonseed oil, high fructose corn syrup, artificial butter flavor, carrageenan, maltodextrin, dehydrated mushrooms, cellulose, carrot powder and artificial crab flavor? I did. And it wasn't pleasant. Let me explain.

I had the pleasure of speaking at an event in St. Augustine Beach last week. They were just completing an eight-part series on Ethical Eating and I spoke about healthy cooking. I was the last presenter and thought the event was very successful. Of course, I figure any event where no one hurls anything at me while I'm speaking is a successful event.

But I digress…

During the course of my cooking demo, I held up a box of Crab-Stuffed Sole that I purchased in the frozen food section of my local grocery store. It promised to be a quick, healthy entrée for two. It even boasted, "Original Classic Recipe", on the front. It sold for just over six bucks, which isn't exactly cheap. I usually don't buy my seafood in fancy blue cardboard boxes, but hey—I'm one to try anything once. Just ask my wife. (But please don't bring up that night with the Cool Whip, hula-hoops, bungee cords, and that thing you have to plug in).

Anyway…this frozen food entrée wasn't all that quick. (For something to qualify as 'quick' for me, I have to be able to do it faster than I can spell it). This dish needed 35 minutes in the oven. When you add ten minutes to preheat the oven you'd be pushing 45 minutes. So I crossed 'quick' off my list of adjectives.

But it had sole and crab, so it must be healthy, right? I thought so 'til I read the ingredient list. Oops. There was no crab in this meal. Just surimi…imitation crab. Worse still, it had no sole. (There's no sole in American waters. True sole must be flown in from Great Britain or Scandinavia, and is, therefore, pretty pricey. What we call sole here in the states is most likely flounder.) But this particular entrée had neither sole nor flounder. It contained fish all right, but an unnamed variety of whitefish probably caught in trawling nets the size of Rhode Island somewhere north of the Bering Sea. Either that or was snatched out of a fish farm somewhere in the bowels of Thailand.

Okay, so my box of crab-stuffed sole entrée had no crab and no sole in it. But it did contain a list of 50+ other ingredients including tetrasodium pyrophosphate.

I don't know about you, but I try not to eat anything with the word 'pyro' in it because I think of pyrotechnics, pyromaniacs, funeral pyres…it's just not an appetizing word. I also try to avoid food with the word 'phosphate' in it. (Didn't we wash our clothes in phosphate detergent back in the 90's before they banned it?)

I have to give them credit on one account, however. They did include calcium carbonate in the ingredients, which, as we all know, is an antacid. TUMS or Rolaids to be exact. See, they must've figured all these chemicals and artificial ingredients would make us sick, so they mixed in some antacid as a pre-emptive strike. No wonder I didn't get an upset stomach.

I had to chuckle as I finished reading the many unpronounceable, laboratory-sounding ingredients and remembered the, "Original Classic Recipe", claim on the cover of the box. Whose "Original Classic Recipe" is this, anyway? Dr. Frankenstein's? Bon appétit, Igor.

Now here's a recipe that contains real seafood, eight other ingredients and can be made in well under half an hour. I've left out the phosphates and TUMS. Oh, and there's not a 'pyro' in sight.

• CRAB STUFFED SOLE •
(Not From a Box)

PREP: 10 minutes   COOK: 30 minutes

INGREDIENTS

2 (4 to 6 ounce) sole, flounder or tilapia fillets

1/2 cup seasoned bread crumbs

1 (6-ounce) can crabmeat - drained and flaked

2 tablespoons finely chopped onion

1 egg, lightly beaten

1/4 teaspoon kosher salt

Dash cayenne pepper

1-1/2 tablespoons unsalted butter, melted)

1-1/2 teaspoons all-purpose flour

1/4 cup clam juice or chicken broth

2 tablespoons grated Parmesan cheese

Paprika to garnish

DIRECTIONS

1. Preheat oven to 350°.

2. Combine breadcrumbs, crab, onion, egg, salt and cayenne in a small bowl. Spoon onto fillets; roll up and secure with a toothpick. Place in a greased baking dish; drizzle with half the butter. Bake, uncovered for 25-30 minutes or until fish flakes easily with a fork.

3. Meanwhile, for sauce, place remaining butter in a small saucepan. Add in flour and stir until smooth. Gradually add broth. Bring to a boil; cook and stir for 2 minutes or until thickened and bubbly.

4. When fish is cooked, spoon sauce over fillets then sprinkle with cheese. Broil 5 inches from the heat until the cheese is melted. Discard the toothpicks, sprinkle with paprika, and serve.

• SAUTÉED CARROTS IN HONEY BUTTER •

PREP: 10 minutes   COOK: 10 minutes

INGREDIENTS
  2 large carrots, peeled and cut into matchsticks
  1 tablespoon honey
  1-1/2 teaspoons frozen apple juice concentrate, thawed
  1 tablespoon and 1-1/2 teaspoons minced fresh parsley
  2 tablespoons chopped toasted hazelnuts
  1/8 teaspoon garlic powder
  1/8 teaspoon ground nutmeg
  1/4 teaspoon salt
  1/8 teaspoon fresh ground pepper
  2 tablespoons unsalted butter

DIRECTIONS
  1. Steam the carrots in a steamer basket over 1 inch of boiling water for 7 to 10
      minutes until tender but still firm.

  2. Meanwhile, in a medium bowl, combine the honey, apple juice concentrate,
      parsley, and hazelnuts. Season with garlic powder, nutmeg, salt and pepper.
      Add the carrots and stir to coat.

  3. Heat butter in a 10-inch skillet over medium-high heat. Add the carrots and
      sauté until heated through.

• BOILED NEW POTATOES WITH BUTTER •

PREP: 5 minutes   COOK: 10 minutes

INGREDIENTS
   1/2-pound small new potatoes
   5 cloves garlic, peeled and cut in half
   1 bay leaf
   1/2 teaspoon whole black peppercorns
   2 teaspoons kosher salt
   2 tablespoons unsalted butter
   Fresh ground pepper to taste

DIRECTIONS
   1.   Place potatoes, garlic, bay leaf and peppercorns in a medium saucepan.
        Add cold water to cover by 1-inch. Bring to a boil over high heat and add a 2
        teaspoons salt. Lower heat and simmer until potatoes are fork-tender, about
        5 - 8 minutes.

   2.   Drain and discard garlic, bay leaf, and peppercorns. Cut the potatoes in half
        and toss with butter, pepper and additional salt to taste.

CHAPTER 18

LET YOUR SMILE BE YOUR UMBRELLA. BUT IF IT'S RAINING, YOU BETTER GET A REAL ONE

A friend of mine recently told me about a whimsical encounter she had with a helpful police officer on a bustling Manhattan street. After she finished she mentioned how our lives are so often filled with encounters wrapped up in BS that we tend to overlook those precious moments suffused with true human contact.

Hearing about her experience reminded me of one of my own. A few years back I was in Chicago for business and found myself ambling up Michigan Avenue on a lovely early-spring afternoon. There was still a chill in the air, but one could easily notice the flower buds struggling to make their way skyward in the planters that lined the avenue.

Suddenly, enormous clouds rolled in from Lake Michigan and the sky opened, sending rain down in torrents. I ducked into a nearby shop and purchased an umbrella. You know the kind - like the one grandma used to own: black with a gnarled wooden handle and large enough to shade a Buick. I thought I was going to get gouged, but I think it only cost me seven bucks. I paid the cashier then stepped back out onto the sidewalk and made my way south toward the river. As people scurried in and out of doorways and taxis, I offered them a space beneath my umbrella. Not a single person turned me down.

I know I couldn't have gotten away with this in New York. I probably would've been punched, knifed, or had the umbrella wrenched from my hands and broken in half over an angry thigh. Heck, the men would've treated me even worse.

But the City of Big Shoulders is different. It's more human and down to earth than NYC. Chicago is an ideal place for an out-of-town Florida boy to offer his umbrella to complete strangers.

So I spent the better part of the afternoon under my cheap canopy chatting with folks I may never have met under other circumstances. Dozens of temporary friends and lively conversations. I'm a richer man because of the time I spent under that umbrella.

Flash forward to the present: We've had lots of rain this month. Six inches this week alone. Unfortunately, I haven't had the pleasure of parading up and down Michigan

Avenue. I've been stuck doing more mundane things: finishing a book, shopping for new tires, testing recipes, wiring a duplex, presenting some cooking demos at a food & wine festival or two, getting used to my new, living arrangements.

Some of it has been fun. Some of it's been a struggle.

But still I find time to smile.

Even if I can't find that damned umbrella.

PS. How do you fare amid the dog days of summer? Well, here's a classic sangria recipe that I promise will bring you a smile as big as an umbrella. I know it did me!

• PERFECT SUMMER SANGRIA •

INGREDIENTS
    1 bottle (750 ml) red wine: Rioja, Merlot, Shiraz, or a Cab

    1/2 cup triple sec or Cointreau

    1/2 cup brandy (optional)

    Juice of one orange (3 tablespoons)

    Juice of one lemon (3 tablespoons)

    Juice of one lime (3 tablespoons)

    2 tablespoons sugar

    1 orange, thinly sliced

    1 lemon, thinly sliced

    1 lime, thinly sliced

    1 cup strawberries or raspberries or a combination of both

    1 8-ounce can diced pineapple with juice

    4 cups ginger ale

DIRECTIONS
1. Mix the wine, triple sec, brandy, citrus juices, and sugar in a large pitcher. Refrigerate overnight.

2. Immediately before serving, stir in the orange, lemon, and lime slices, strawberries, pineapple and ginger ale. Serve over ice.

CHAPTER 19

RESTAURANTS YOU MIGHT VISIT JUST SO YOU CAN STEAL SOMETHING WITH THEIR NAME ON IT

I'm fortunate to be able to travel around the state of Florida meeting new folks and taking in the local cuisine. In doing so, I'm often tickled by the names of the restaurants I stumble across.

Some are classy, some are creative, and some just make you scratch your head and say, "*Huh?*"

Since I always carry a pen and notepad in the car with me (for those rare moments when I have an idea worth keeping) I started to jot down some of the more unusual restaurant names. I even included the cities in case you want to drop by and filch a menu or mug when you're in the neighborhood.

Chinee Takee Outee (Jacksonville) - I love Chinese food and I love any restaurant whose name invokes the mysteries of the Orient. This little dive certainly does because it's a mystery as to why any sane restaurateur would pay good money to set up a joint and then name it this. Unless, of course, the owner relocated here from the hills of West Virginia, at which point his stab at the Chinese language makes complete sense. But every time I drive by, I have to smile.

Gas (St. Augustine) - I imagine they decided to adopt this moniker because the building may have been an old gas station. Perhaps it was. But the place has had so many tenants and has undergone so many renovations over the years that any semblance of a gas station is long gone. Sorta like welding two wheels onto a horse then calling it a bicycle. But let me tell you, the food is awesome there.

Pho King Noodle House (Jacksonville) - Not really sure what to make of this one, but I hope the noodles are good. I mean really good. Because this isn't just any noodle house, this is The *Pho King* Noodle House.

Fu King Restaurant (Lake City) - Another Oriental restaurant with a name that leaves little to the imagination. Good thing these guys aren't located in Jacksonville. Then they'd be duking it out with the Noodle House for the title of best Fu King restaurant in Jax.

Dogwater Café (Clearwater) - This name is about as unappetizing as they get, especially for those of us who've spent time among dogs. I mean, what were they thinking? Was "The Litterbox Brasserie" already taken?

Dirty Dicks Crab House (Panama City) - Another one that defies explanation. I don't know about you, but I make it a point to steer clear of any restaurant whose name includes both unhygienic reproductive organs *and* a parasitical venereal disease.

Phylthy Phils Waterfront Cafe (St. Pete Beach) - Not as bad as Dirty Dicks. But not much better, either. Besides, word on the street says that Phil has crabs, too.

Gassey Jacks (Orange City) - Not to be outdone by the St. Augustine restaurant with the similar name, this establishment at least has the integrity to identify the guy responsible for all the gas.

Better than Sex (Key West) - I ate there. It's not.

Lulu's Bra and Grill (Fernandina Beach) - Methinks the guy they hired to paint the sign for this popular joint started in on the project after downing a couple of six packs. Since the restaurant was just starting out and probably didn't have the cash to redo the sign, they just let it ride. The rest is history.

Mema's Alaskan Tacos (Tampa) - Nothing gets one's saliva running like the smell of grilled beef, sizzling onions and sautéed chilies wrapped up in a warm, cheese-filled tortilla. And who better to create this delectable south-of-the-border creation than those who have honed this culinary craft over the centuries. That's right: the Aleuts. Nobody dishes up better tortillas, refried beans and frosty margaritas than those who tramped across the Bering Strait only to settle in a state that is best known for grizzly bears, ice cubes and goofy politicians.

Molly Goodhead's (Ozona) - For some reason this place has been popular since day one. Of course it caters mainly to rising CEO's, professional athletes from the visiting team, and members of the construction trades. Although, occasionally, some beefy girl on a Harley has been known to stop by. Don't know what that's all about.

B. O.'s Fish Wagon (Key West) - Any eating establishment that has B.O. in the title is worth driving by. And because it looks like dump, that's exactly what most people do. But the food is very good. And here's the deal: if you go to B.O.'s for lunch, be sure to ask for the 'Daily Special.' Doing so will get you a sandwich far below the price they charge for tourists. Shhh. Don't tell anyone.

Cheap (Tampa) - You gotta give 'em credit. At least they're honest.

Junk Food Jacks (Clearwater) - Another joint with the integrity to own up to what really comes out of the kitchen.

O'Boobigan's (Clearwater) - When the first Hooter's opened on Gulf to Bay Blvd some twenty-odd years ago, who could've predicted the impact it'd have on the culinary world. Soon dozens of copy cat "breastaurants" began popping up all over Pinellas County to cash in on the Hooter's vibe: Melons, Headlights, Knockers, Mugs & Jugs, O'Boobigans... Alas, only a few remain. O'Boobigan's Irish Pub is one of them. (Personally, I've never been much of a frequenter of these mammary-influenced establishments. As far as I'm concerned, if you've seen one, you've seen 'em both...)

So...this is what we have down our way. What are some funny restaurant names in your neck of the woods? Jot 'em down and send them along.

And while you're doing that, let's look at some "Restaurant Recipes" that you can make at home. Places like Panera Bread Company, Applebee's, or Red Lobster. I've never worked in any of these joints so the recipes that follow aren't the exact ones that they use.

However, they are pretty close. The nice thing? The ingredients, for the most part, are fresh. You can also control the sodium and you can tweak them as much as your heart desires. Heck, you may never eat out again (except maybe to steal a menu from a creatively named establishment.)

• BROCCOLI CHEESE SOUP •

This will make enough for 4 servings, so save the rest for lunch the next day.

PREP: 10 minutes   COOK: 50 minutes

INGREDIENTS
  1/4 cup plus 1 tablespoon unsalted butter, divided
  1 medium onion, finely chopped
  1 clove garlic, minced
  1/4 cup all purpose flour
  2 cups half and half (or 2 cups evaporated milk)
  2 cups chicken broth
  8 ounces broccoli, chopped (may be fresh or frozen)
  1 cup finely chopped carrots
  1/4 teaspoon nutmeg
  Kosher salt and freshly ground pepper to taste
  2 cups grated sharp cheddar cheese (8 ounces)
  2 bread bowls (optional)

DIRECTIONS
  1. Melt 1 tablespoon butter in a skillet over medium-high heat. Add onions and
      sauté until soft and translucent, about 8 minutes. Add garlic and sauté one
      more minute.

  2. Melt 1/4 cup butter in a medium sauce pan over medium heat. Sprinkle in
      flour and whisk for 4 or 5 minutes. Slowly add half and half, whisking until it's
      well mixed. Slowly add chicken broth and whisk until thickened. Lower heat
      and simmer for 20 minutes.

  3. Add broccoli, carrots and sautéed onions. Continue to cook over low heat
      until vegetables are tender, about 10 minutes or so. Season with kosher salt
      and freshly ground pepper to taste.

  4. Pour half the mixture into a blender and puree until smooth. Pour into bowl
      and add the remaining mixture to the blender and puree.

  5. Return both purees to the saucepan and stir the cheese and nutmeg. Cook
      over low heat, stirring until the cheese is melted.

Pour into warm bowls or bread bowls. Serve with warm crusty bread.

• GRILLED CHICKEN ORIENTAL SALAD •

PREP: 10 minutes   COOK: 10 minutes

FOR THE DRESSING:

1/4 cup mayonnaise

4 tablespoons rice wine vinegar

2 tablespoons sugar

2 tablespoons sesame seed oil

1 teaspoon toasted sesame seed oil

1 teaspoon Dijon mustard

DIRECTIONS

Combine the sugar, and rice wine vinegar in a medium bowl and mix until sugar is dissolved. Stir in remaining ingredients until well blended.

FOR THE SALAD:

2 boneless, skinless chicken breasts

1 tablespoon olive or canola oil

1/2 cup crispy rice noodles

1/2 cup sliced almonds

2 tablespoons shredded carrots

Kosher salt and freshly ground pepper to taste

4 cups romaine lettuce or mixed greens

DIRECTIONS

1. Place each chicken breast between two pieces of wax paper and pound until around 1/4-inch thick.

2. Heat olive oil in a 10-inch skillet over medium-high heat. Add chicken breasts and cook for 4 minutes per side. Remove to a warm plate.

3. Meanwhile, place almonds in a small skillet over medium heat and cook until lightly toasted. Remove to a layer of paper towels.

4. Slice chicken into thin strips. Place half the lettuce on each plate and top with shredded carrots, rice noodles, almonds and sliced chicken. Pour dressing over all and serve.

• BACON WRAPPED SCALLOPS •

PREP: 5 minutes   MARINATE: 30 minutes

COOK: 15 minutes

INGREDIENTS

1 pound dry sea scallops (12 - 16)

6 - 8 slices bacon, cut in half (to equal amount of scallops)

6 tablespoons unsalted butter

1/3 cup dry white wine (i.e. Sauvignon Blanc)

2 teaspoons fresh lemon juice

1/2 teaspoon Hungarian paprika

1/2 teaspoon seasoned salt

DIRECTIONS

1. Preheat oven to 400°.

2. Meanwhile, melt butter in a small saucepan over medium heat. Add wine, paprika, seasoned salt, and lemon juice. Stir until salt dissolves. Pour into a bowl and let cool a bit. Add scallops, toss and let marinate for 30 minutes while the oven heats.

3. Pat scallops dry, then wrap a piece of bacon around each one and secure with a toothpick. Place on a lightly greased baking sheet and cook for 10 minutes. Turn and continue to cook until bacon is barely crisp, about 5 minutes more.

CHAPTER 20

SOMETIMES WHAT I READ ABOUT SALT IS NOT WORTH ITS...WELL...SALT

Whenever I'm doing a cooking show or book signing, a number of people can be counted on to ask if my recipes are low-salt.

But they rarely ask if my recipes contain too much celery, paprika, or include ingredients that might impinge upon the rights of an overly sensitive people group.

No. Salt is the issue of today. Granted, I still have a few people who ask if my recipes are low in fat - but that's rare since the low-fat craze has lost a lot of oomph.

So why is salt such a big issue? Because the over-use of salt has been linked to such maladies as high blood pressure, stomach cancer, asthma, Alzheimer's, kidney stones, osteoporosis and, according to one report I found while leafing through a recent edition of *Cars, Guns and Chicks* magazine when I was getting my oil changed, it may also be responsible for those morons in front of us who drive with their blinkers on even though they have no intention of turning.

Think about it. We've all seen articles and books with alarming titles like: *Salt: The Pillar of Death,* or *The Saline Silent Killer,* or *I Was a Salt-Licking Teenage Mutant from the Planet Sodium.*

Yes, salt's getting a bad rap these days. So let me help set the record straight*.

Salt, like money, is not evil. (Actually, the statement is: The *love of* money is the root of all evil.)

It's not even dangerous. (Too much or too little can be harmful, but that goes for just about anything).

Our bodies need salt. We can't function without it. But hey, I'm not going to go on and on expounding on the biological reasons as to why this is the case. That's why God created science textbooks.

No, I'm not here to teach a science lesson. Nor am I here to insist that our consumption of salt is not harmful. I believe, and the data shows, that Americans do ingest too much. So we should cut back. But not necessarily in our day-to-day cooking. Why? Because salt does affect flavor. In a big way.

The 1/2-teaspoon of salt that we stir into a sauce or sprinkle on a steak would be sorely missed if we were to ban it from our cupboards. No, this thoughtful and moderate use of salt is not the primary culprit in our struggle with hypertension or any or the other maladies listed above.

The real culprit? Processed food. Most are loaded with salt. Look at the label of any processed food to see what I mean. If you want to cut down on your sodium intake, cut down on your intake of processed food. I also steer clear of fast food and family-style restaurants as a matter of habit because they also load their dishes with salt.

So, unless you're strictly advised otherwise by your physician, feel free to sprinkle some kosher salt on that roast, vegetable, or starch. Your body won't mind and your taste buds will love you.

I use all-purpose table salt in many everyday applications, especially baking, because the small grains dissolve readily. But I'll reach for kosher salt when seasoning meat, fish, poultry or vegetables because it's easier to control and the larger grains cling a bit better. It's also great for tweaking a dish because I can pick a pinch up with my fingers very easily. So I keep a bowl of kosher salt next to my stove for just that purpose.

Oh, and on a side note, have you ever wondered why a number of chefs (including me) sprinkle kosher salt on a dish from a height of 12 to 20 inches? It's not because we want to look cool (Hopefully the food we prepare will showcase our talent.) No, the reason we sprinkle salt from such a height is because it's more evenly distributed that way. Go ahead. Try it. And the fact that it looks cool certainly doesn't hurt, either.

So we've touched on some of the issues of salt. But there's more. Topics like: How and when is it best to apply salt. Are there any advantages to salt grinders? Why the current rage over sea salt? I address these topics and more in my book *Table for Two - The Kitchen Companion*. But for now, I'll show you a great way to make your meat more succulent and flavorful.

Now, pass the salt, will ya?

*As a matter of record, I'm not a nutritionist, dietitian or doctor (although I once played doctor with the other kids when I was a child). The recommendations made in this book are the result of careful study and research. So please consult your physician to see if you need to limit your salt intake.

BRINING: THE KEY TO FLAVORFUL AND SUCCULENT MEAT

Why are some turkeys, chickens and pork roasts as dry as the Sahara, when others turn out melt-in-your-mouth juicy? One word: brining. Soaking a turkey, chicken or pork roast in a solution of kosher salt, sugar and water provides it with a plump cushion of seasoned moisture that will sustain it throughout cooking. Without going into a lot of scientific detail, brining works through diffusion and osmosis. The salt and sugar move from the brine into the cells of the meat (diffusion) as well as the water (osmosis). This process causes the cell proteins to unravel and prevents them from interacting with each other. When this occurs, a sticky matrix is formed that will keep the moisture from leaking out when the meat begins to cook, thus creating a wonderfully tender and seasoned entree.

But enough science. The bottom line is that it works. And here's how it's done:

BASIC BRINE FOR TURKEY, CHICKEN AND PORK PER POUND OF FOOD (NOT TO EXCEED 2 GALLONS):

1 quart cold water per pound of food

1/2 cup Diamond Crystal kosher Salt, or 1/4 cup plus 2 tablespoons Morton's kosher Salt, or 1/4 cup table salt per quart

1/2 cup sugar per quart

Time: 1 hour per pound, no more than 8 hours

BRINE FOR HIGH-HEAT ROASTING OR GRILLING PER POUND
(NOT TO EXCEED 2 GALLONS):

1 quart cold water per pound of food

1/4 cup Diamond Crystal kosher salt, or 3 tablespoons Morton kosher salt, or 2 tablespoons salt per quart

2 tablespoons sugar per quart

Time: 1 hour per pound, no more than 8 hours.

DIRECTIONS:
1. Bring 2 cups water to a boil and add salt and sugar to dissolve. Remove from heat and let cool. Add remaining water and refrigerate until cold.

2. Place the meat or fish into a plastic bag that is large enough to hold the brine and the meat. Refrigerate for the allotted time. For larger cuts, like turkey, place in a cooler, add brine and frozen ice packs to ensure that the brine remains at 40°.

3. Remove meat or fish. Pat dry and cook according to directions. For crisp skin on turkeys or chickens, air dry on a rack in your refrigerator.

SUGGESTED BRINING TIMES FOR TYPICAL MEATS AND SEAFOOD:

Shrimp: 30 Minutes

Pork Chops: 1 - 2 hours

Cornish Hens: 1 to 2 hours

Pork Tenderloin (whole): 3 - 4 hours

Whole Pork Loin: 6 - 8 hours

Whole Chicken (4 to 5 pounds): 3 - 4 hours

Turkey (12 to 14 pounds): 8 hours

CHAPTER 21

HOW ARE FROZEN VEGGIES IN SAUCE LIKE COUNT DRACULA? THEY BOTH SUCK

Okay. Maybe I'm overstating my case. Let me backtrack.

I love frozen vegetables.

Really. I do.

I recommend them as a viable (and sometimes better) alternative to the fresh vegetables in the produce section when the fresh veggies are under-ripe or way past their prime. In that case, frozen veggies, because they are picked and frozen right after harvesting, may provide better flavor and nutrients than some of the items you find in the produce section.

Of course, I realize that some frozen veggies don't translate well in the "crispness" department (think broccoli, squash, carrots), but if you're looking for healthy vegetables without added salt or preservatives, frozen is the way to go. Besides, they can be uber-affordable if you buy them when your supermarket offers a buy-one-get-one-free special.

Segue: Check this out. In our local supermarket, the lights in the frozen food display cases don't turn on until someone approaches them. Is that cool or what? I know they do it to save electricity, but for those of us without television, it's truly a fun night out. I remember how my kids would jump all over, begging me to take them to the grocery store so they could run up and down the aisle and play with the lights. It was a lot like playing gooney golf except there were no golf clubs, large dinosaurs, or that frumpy guy behind the register watching wrestling on cable TV.

Now where was I? Oh yeah. So why do I say frozen veggies-in-sauce suck?

Here's why.

I recently realized that my local supermarket's frozen veggie section has been going through a metamorphosis. At one time the freezer shelves were filled with bags and bags of 16-ounce frozen veggies from a half-dozen different producers: Bird's Eye®, Green Giant®, PictSweet®, McKenzies®, the store brand, etc. But lately I've noticed that these same shelves of plain veggies are being crowded out by newer offerings: 12-ounce bags with all matter of sauces and spices added. Oh, and then there's the newest kid on the block: 12-ounce steam-in-the bag veggies. Here's how one national brand describes them:

"A specially designed bag and advanced steaming technology, it's a revolutionary way to prepare perfectly cooked vegetables, rice and pasta blends right in your microwave."

My question? I had no trouble perfectly cooking the old version of frozen vegetables by nuking them in the microwave or steaming them on the stove, so why create something new? Could it be that these companies want to charge us more money for less product? Hmmm. What's so revolutionary about that? (Remember when canned tomatoes were 16 ounces or when ice cream came in half-gallon containers?)

So, I guess I'll head down to the grocery store and stock up on a few cases of the pre-revolutionary frozen vegetables. You may want to do the same.

Then one day we can let our grandkids crawl up on our knees while we pine about the olden days, when 16-ounce bags of frozen vegetables were exactly just that: frozen vegetables. This is one time when I won't join the masses out on the street to chant "Vive la revolution!"

FROZEN VEGGIES I ALWAYS HAVE ON HAND:

Peas: I never buy fresh. Too much work! And frozen peas never disappoint.

Corn: not corn on the cob. For that I always opt for fresh. Corn doesn't freeze well on the cob.

Lima Beans: See peas.

Pearl Onions: See peas.

Spinach: Fresh takes up too much room in my fridge. I only buy fresh for salads.

Mixed Veggies (Corn, string beans, carrots): Lot's of nutrition in this. Great to add to soups, too!

Peas & Carrots: See mixed veggies.

Succotash: See mixed veggies.

Broccoli: Fresh broccoli degrades quickly, so I opt for fresh unless I'm stir frying, then I buy a bag of florets in the produce section.

Cauliflower: See broccoli.

FROZEN VEGGIES I'D USE IN A PINCH:

Carrots: fresh carrots keep well, are inexpensive, and I can use what I need.

String beans: I really like fresh because I like them a little crunchy.

Brussels Sprouts: Like string beans, I like them a bit crunch so I get them fresh. But they are very seasonal so I keep some frozen on hand. I don't defrost them before cooking (they become too mushy) so I just toss the frozen babies with some olive oil and roast them 'til they brown and have a nice crunch, about 30 minutes or so.

Asparagus: Like string beans, I like my asparagus a tad crunchy. But they, too, are seasonal. Sigh.

VEGGIES I NEVER BUY FROZEN:

Onions: they're cheap and available year round. Frozen have neither the flavor nor the texture of non-frozen.

Red or green peppers: Frozen peppers will always come out soft and wilted regardless of how you cook them. I opt for fresh.

Yellow squash or zucchini: Like peppers, they will always come out super soft regardless of how you prepare them.

Vegetable medleys for stir frying: You want your veggies crisp-tender in a stir fry. You aren't going to get crisp-tender from frozen veggies. Best to get a bag of pre-packaged medley from the produce department.

Mushrooms: Like onions, they're cheap and are available year round. Plus, you can sauté them as faster than you can frozen.

• SIMPLE CHEDDAR CHEESE SAUCE •

INGREDIENTS
   1 tablespoon unsalted butter
   1 tablespoon all-purpose flour
   2/3 cup milk
   1 cup freshly grated cheddar cheese
   Kosher salt and freshly ground pepper to taste

DIRECTIONS
Melt butter in a saucepan over medium heat. Whisk in flour until smooth. Slowly add milk into butter mixture, whisking constantly. Cook and stir until mixture thickens, about 3 minutes. Add cheddar cheese and stir until cheese is melted, about 3 additional minutes. Season with salt and pepper.

CHAPTER 22
WHEN LIFE HANDS YOU LEMONADE...ADD VODKA

When I moved across state for the first time a few years ago, I thought it'd be my "last move". Not to be confused with my previous 'last move' a couple of years before that. A move that took me within a block of the beach.

I opted to move from St. Augustine to the Tampa Bay area because of work. Not that I can write books any better on the west coast of Florida as opposed to the east coast. Heck, I can mangle the English language just as well on either coast, thank you very much.

No. This had more to do with the fact that I was doing most of my in-state cooking demonstrations on the west coast.

Why?

Demographics.

There are a gazillion more empty-nesters and young married couples in the Tampa Bay area alone (not even counting Sarasota, Venice or Naples) compared to Northeast Florida. Heck, I was already making the trek across the state 6 or 8 times a month as it was. By moving to the west coast, I save a butt load on travel and hotel expenses.

Plus, I don't have to crawl through that 8-lane Orlando parking lot the locals euphemistically refer to as I-4.

So, yeah, the move was work-related.

But also family related. My Mom was pushing 80 at the time, and as every good Irishman knows, you gotta look after family.

Since there was no way in heck that Mom would move into the little beach house with me, I loaded up a big old truck and crawled across the state, putting most of my stuff in storage before moving back into the huge 4 bedroom house in which I'd spent most of my high school years.

Lot's of memories there.

And lots of work that needed to be done.

My mom might've been up there in years, but she was extremely self-reliant. So there was a number of projects she'd planned on getting around to but just hadn't yet: Like re-grouting the shower in the guest bathroom, replacing the exterior doors, and hauling my younger brother's Mustang exhaust system up to the attic until he had a chance to come and fetch it. So I had my hands full house-wise.

But moving in with family can require some adjustments. Here are just a few:

The stove had only one working burner. It seems odd that someone like me who writes cookbooks for a living would abide a stove with only one burner for even a day, let alone months, but trust me, that first week there was a lot more to do. Like unpack. So I had to be creative. For the first four or five days, I made some great one-pot meals. (I've listed one such dish below.) Oh, and did I mention that my cookware was still packed? So I had to use whatever mom still had lying around. Told you I had to get creative.

The microwave was useless. No, it wasn't broken. In fact, it looked brand new. I think it was one of the first incarnations. It was just too small and inefficient. How inefficient? I put a bag of Orville Redenbacher popcorn in as I settled down to watch a Civil War documentary on cable. The popcorn didn't finish popping until Lee surrendered at Appomattox. I replaced her microwave with mine. (Unlike my pots and pans, my microwave was fairly accessible.)

The air conditioning was always off. Oh, it worked all right. In fact it was just replaced. But Mom liked it warm. Really warm. Heck, the popcorn popped faster leaving it out on the counter than it did in her tiny microwave. At first I thought about going "au naturel". I suppose that might've been pretty cool in my 20's. But at my age? I think not. Solution? I closed all the vents in Mom's part of the house and opened all the vents in my side of the house. Problem solved. And no one had to go naked.

But it wasn't all bad. There's an ultra-cool downtown area just down the road (in fact, there are dozens of great downtown areas within a short drive) and the Gulf beaches are spectacular. The bike trails are close, the restaurants are hip, the sunset never fails, and the vodka is cheap.

After all, if life serves you lemonade, you gotta add the vodka.

Especially if it's family.

Because if you can't roll with the punches, you're gonna get knocked out.

• SECOND CITY WHITE BEAN CHILI •

I call this Second City Chili not because it was created in Chicago, but because this is the essence of culinary improv. I found a few cans of this and that in the pantry, some chicken breasts in the freezer, and some assorted spices in the cupboard. This was the result. I'm not sure if I remembered all the ingredients but it just may inspire you to pull off a little improv yourself. Who knows? You may find yourself in a kitchen with only one working burner, too. Enjoy!

PREP: 10 minutes   COOK: 35 minutes

INGREDIENTS
- 2 tablespoons olive or canola oil
- 1 large onion, chopped (about 1 cup)
- 2 cloves garlic, minced or pressed
- 1/2 teaspoon dried oregano
- 1 tablespoon chili powder (or more or less to taste)
- 1 teaspoon ground cumin
- 2 cups chicken broth
- 1 (16-ounce) can diced tomatoes
- 1 7-ounce can diced green chilies
- 1 (16-ounce) can creamed corn
- 1 pound diced, cooked chicken meat
- 2 (15-ounce) cans northern beans
- Kosher salt and freshly ground pepper to taste
- Hot pepper sauce to taste (I like Frank's)
- Grated sharp Cheddar cheese, to garnish

DIRECTIONS
1. Heat oil in a dutch oven over medium-high heat. Add onions and sauté until soft and translucent, about 8 minutes. Add garlic and sauté 1 minute. Add oregano, cumin and chili powder and sauté 3 additional minutes.

2. Stir in broth, tomatoes and chilies. Bring to a boil, lower heat, and then simmer for 10 minutes.

3. Add corn, chicken and beans and simmer for 10 minutes. Season with salt, pepper and hot sauce to taste. Sprinkle with cheese and serve.

CHAPTER 23

CINCO DE MAYO, BUT HOLD THE MAYO

Happy Cinco de Mayo, everyone! While not the largest south-of-the border celebration - that would probably be *Dieciséis de Septiembre* (Mexico's Independence Day) - Cinco de Mayo sure is a lot easier to pronounce if you happen to be a non-Spanish speaker. Especially after a few margaritas.

Cinco de Mayo commemorates the victory of the outnumbered Mexican Militia over the French Army at the Battle of Puebla in 1862. Brave Mexican warriors entered the fray shouting their three-fold battle cry *"Viva Mexico!"* (Translated: Long live Mexico) while the French, sensing impending defeat, responded with a battle cry of their own, *"Oh non pas encore!"* (translated: Oh no, not again).

Interestingly enough, Cinco de Mayo is pretty much a regional holiday in Mexico and is primarily celebrated in the state of Puebla. In the United States, however, it has fast become a major holiday celebration throughout much of the country.

Of course, Americans are always open to new ethnic expressions of celebration – especially if a lot of drinking is involved. Which is one reason why Congress just recently recognized *Reddition Française* (French Surrender Day), which may be celebrated any day when you have too much beer in the fridge.

But back to Cinco de Mayo. Festival Broadway is considered the primo Cinco de Mayo celebration in the world. This event, held in an eleven block area of downtown Los Angeles, welcomes over half a million people where shouts of *"Viva Mexico!* (Long live Mexico), *"Dios bendice México"* (God bless Mexico), and *"Averigüe los nuevos rines en mi Cívico!"* (Check out the new rims on my Civic) fill the air.

In Scottsdale, Arizona, the Rawhide Wild West Town celebrates Cinco de Mayo with an annual running of the bulls. However, this may be a dying tradition. According to spokesperson Gimpy Delgado, the insurance rates for Goring-by-Bull have skyrocketed since that unfortunate death last year in Pamplona when a 30-year-old tourist was gored in the throat. Especially so since the man was taking a shower in his hotel room at the time.

Not to be outdone by the event in Scottsdale, the town of Chandler hosts the Running of the Chihuahuas. This cultural classic features over 150 pint-sized dogs racing for the ultimate canine prize: a tasty biscuit and a pat on the head. While not as dangerous as her sister event in Scottsdale, the Running of the Chihuahuas does produce a number of nipped ankles and more than a few humped legs.

And in San Diego, you can down your share of margaritas at the Cinco de Mayo Zonkey Fest where the Zonkey – a small pony that looks like a donkey and is painted with zebra stripes – holds court. I don't know about you, but it seems to me the idea of painting zebra stripes on a pony could only have been hatched during a previous margarita-soaked Cinco de Mayo celebration.

So…how are you celebrating Cinco de Mayo? Me? I'm gonna party with friends, load a cooler full of Dos Equis beer, whip up a huge a pitcher of margaritas, and cook up platters of homemade fish tacos. Hold the mayo.

• ALMOST CLASSIC FISH TACOS •

Most classic fish taco recipes call for deep-fried battered fish. They also require a good bit of mayonnaise and sour cream or yogurt. But it doesn't have to be so. In fact, I prefer this version. Not only is it healthier, but the clean-up is much easier. If you don't have the time or inclination to grill these babies, you can pan sear the fillets indoors. I also forgo the lettuce and used bagged shredded cabbage, instead. I do this for a couple of reasons. One, if you're only cooking for 2 (or 4 or 6), it doesn't make sense to buy a whole head of lettuce to shred. Two, lettuce is the least nutritious green in the produce department. Three, I can use my cabbage in a variety of soups and stews.

PREP: 10 minutes   COOK: 5 minutes

FOR THE TACOS:

INGREDIENTS

3/4 pound mahi mahi, tuna or swordfish fillets

1 tablespoon olive oil or canola oil

2 teaspoons blackening spice (I like Paul Prudhomme's)

4 corn tortillas

1 cup bagged shredded cabbage

DIRECTIONS

1. Preheat a grill (or 10-inch skillet if cooking inside) over medium-high heat. Brush the fillets with oil and rub on the blackening spice. Place the fish on the grill and cook for 4 minutes. Carefully turn, and cook until the fish flakes with a fork, about 4 more minutes. Transfer to a plate and cover to keep warm.

2. Place the tortillas on the grill for 1 – 2 minutes until soft and pliable (if cooking indoors, wrap the tortillas in a damp paper towel and nuke for 1 minute).

3. Slice the fish and divide amount the tortillas. Top with the cabbage and salsa.

FOR THE SALSA:

INGREDIENTS

    1 mango - peeled, pitted and diced

    1 avocado - peeled, pitted, and diced

    1/2 red onion, diced

    1/2 cup chopped fresh cilantro

    Juice of 1 lime

    Kosher salt and freshly ground pepper to taste

DIRECTIONS

    In a medium bowl, combine the mango, avocado and red onion. Stir in the cilantro, lime juice, salt and pepper. Let sit at room temperature so the flavors meld. Toss once again before using.

CHAPTER 24

WHEN MY MIND WANDERS, IT OFTEN RETURNS WITH SOME GREAT COOKING TIPS

For most of my life I've suffered from migrate headaches.

No. Not migraine.

Migrate.

You see, my mind has a habit of wandering, but occasionally it migrates. Sometimes it migrates so far I often fear I'll lose it. Such was the case this past week.

While my mind was gone, I had some time to reflect. Here's what I realized: I promised my readers timesaving kitchen tips and helpful cooking hints.

See? It's right up there in the book blurb.

Unfortunately, I haven't lived up to my promise.

Sure, I've dished up some winsome commentary, lots of buffoonery, and a couple of good recipes, but there's been a dearth of tips.

But wouldn't you know it? When my mind returned, it had in its possession a bevy of kitchen tips. Here are a good half-dozen, in no particular order.

Enjoy!

Chopping Onions Without Tears
A good way to avoid tears when chopping onions is to put the onion in the freezer a half-hour or so before you chop it. A chilled onion will make you cry less. Then when you're ready to chop, use a razor-sharp knife. If you use a dull knife, instead of slicing through the onion it crushes its way through onion, damaging cells and combining sulfuric compounds and enzymes to create thiopropanal sulfoxide, the substance that irritates our eyes. Plus, with a sharp knife, you'll get your chopping done quicker and won't be hovering over the onion longer than you have to.

Of course, the best way to avoid tears when chopping onions is to have your spouse or kids do it while you go out and get the mail.

Testing the Heat of a Fresh Hot Pepper
You can't test the heat of a pepper just by looking at it. And testing the heat level of a Scotch bonnet, habanero, or even a jalapeño pepper by biting into it is not, and never will be, a good idea, especially at the grocery store.

For some odd reason, shoppers seem to steer clear of produce with bite marks. You'll just have to get it home, chop it, and give it a taste test.

If You Do Burn Your Mouth On a Hot Pepper
Don't reach for a glass of water; it'll only make it worse. Instead, reach for some milk, yogurt or even ice cream. The casein in the dairy products attach themselves to the capsaicinoids in the hot peppers and haul them away (much like dish detergent does to grease).

Soy Sauce, Salt, and the Fifth Taste
Contrary to the opinion of many, soy sauce is not just liquid salt. If you want to add a little 'something' to gravy, soup, or broth, reach for the soy sauce before you reach for the salt. A couple of dashes of soy sauce will add what the Japanese call umami, the fifth taste we can perceive after sweet, sour, salty, and bitter. Give it a shot.

Saving Fresh Herbs
So you bought a bunch of parsley for a recipe that called for 2 teaspoons. What do you do with the rest? One option is to place the remainder in a glass with water covering the roots, then set it in the fridge, replacing the water occasionally. It should keep for a good while. If you don't plan on using a lot in the short term, go ahead and chop all of your parsley (basil, cilantro, sage, etc) and place a tablespoon in each compartment of an ice cube tray. Add just enough water to cover and freeze. Then pop the cubes out into a baggie, label it, and toss it back into the freezer. Now when you need a 'fresh' herb for a stew, soup, sauce or sauté, grab a cube out of the freezer and toss it in. For a little extra pizzazz, freeze the herbs in white wine instead of water.

Sex and Chocolate
If someone declares that a certain brand of chocolate is better than sex, they're lying.

Shameless Plug: I have hundreds of real cooking tips like these I my book *Table for Two – The Kitchen Companion*. It's available online or in fine bookstores everywhere.

CHAPTER 25

LOBSTER MAC & CHEESE? REALLY? WHO CAN AFFORD TO MAKE THIS?

I was appearing at a Food & Wine Fest in Orlando, Florida a few years back and was bewildered by the line that had formed outside a local restaurant's booth. It was twice as long as any other of the lines. I had to find out what the hubbub was all about so I ambled on over. Turns out they were serving one of their signature dishes: lobster mac & cheese.

As a performer they didn't make me wait in line and served me up a nice steaming bowl.

I lifted a spoonful and prepared myself for what must be a dish fit for the gods.

I was underwhelmed.

Don't get me wrong.

I love lobster. I really do.

I grew up on Long Island Sound where most everyone I knew who had a boat had lobster traps. Boat owners probably ate it more often than a lot of folks cuz we could just motor out in our boats and haul up the traps. It was easy to take for granted because we didn't have to pay for it. (Imagine my surprise when I moved to Florida as a teenager and saw what they were charging for those things in the grocery store!)

I also love mac & cheese.

My mom made if from scratch a couple of times a month to feed me, my siblings, and my cousins when we came home from school for lunch. (I know…that's a foreign concept for many nowadays, but back then in Mamaroneck, NY, kids came home for lunch).

But my love for both of these culinary delights doesn't mean that I enjoy seeing them combined into one dish. Particularly with the going rate of lobster meat (like, $50 + dollars a pound).

No, if I'm going to have lobster I want it unadulterated. Maybe a little lemon or drawn butter on the side. I just can't see hiding that wonderfully delicious meat in a bowl of gooey cheese and pasta.

So I still enjoy my lobster and mac & cheese. Just not in the same dish.

But that doesn't mean we can't have some fun tweaking our mac and cheese, right?

First things first, I know the boxed mac & cheese is cheap and easy to make. After all, traditional mac & cheese requires a pre-heated oven, creating a roux, and almost an hour of your time. That's fine if you want to go the traditional route. I often do.

But if I want something I can whip up in about the same amount of time as the boxed version? Sign me up.

Here's a great recipe that you can make stovetop that will beat the pants off the boxed version. You may never go back.

• STOVE TOP MAC & CHEESE •

I know it's convenient to use pre-shredded cheese, and it may work in a pinch, but bagged cheese also has cellulous added to prevent clumping and it won't melt as evenly or easily as freshly grated cheese.

INGREDIENTS:

8 ounces elbow macaroni

8 ounces evaporated milk

2 cups (8 ounces) freshly grated medium cheddar, fontina, Gruyère, or Monterey Jack cheese (or you can mix and match)

Salt and freshly ground pepper to taste

DIRECTIONS:

1. Place macaroni in a medium saucepan and add just enough cold water to cover it. Add a pinch of salt and bring to a boil, stirring frequently. Cook until the water is almost completely absorbed and the macaroni just about al dente, about 7 minutes.

2. Stir in the evaporated milk and bring to a boil. Add the cheese and reduce heat to low. Cook, stirring continuously, until the cheese melts and creates a creamy sauce, about 2 minutes. Season with salt and pepper to taste.

COOKING OUTSIDE THE LINES VARIATIONS

Once you start making these, you'll get other ideas for ramping up your mac & cheese!

Bacon & Hot Sauce Mac & Cheese: add some crumbled bacon, chives and hot sauce to taste after you make your mac & cheese.

Buffalo Chicken Mac & Cheese: Add 1/2 cup diced cooked chicken and 2 tablespoons Franks Hot Sauce (or more to taste) after you make your mac & cheese.

Tuna Mac & Cheese: stir in a can of packed-in-water tuna or salmon after you make your mac & cheese. Make sure you break up the tuna with a fork before adding.

Peas and Mac & Cheese: add a cup of frozen peas to the macaroni when you're cooking it (or nuke them in the microwave and add after you've made the mac & cheese).

Tuna and Peas Mac & Cheese: Heck, why not combine the 2 recipes above?

Broccoli and Mac & Cheese: add a cup of chopped frozen broccoli (or cauliflower) to the macaroni when you're cooking it (or nuke them in the microwave, and add after you've made the mac & cheese).

BLT Mac & Cheese: add crumbled bacon, 1 cup diced tomatoes (if using canned, drain well), and a handful of arugula or baby spinach leaves after you make your mac & cheese.

Ham and Cheese Mac & Cheese: Add a cup of diced cooked ham after you make your mac & cheese.

Tomato and Chili Mac & Cheese: Add 1 cup diced tomatoes and chili powder to taste after you make your mac & cheese.

Shrimp Mac & Cheese: Add 1/3 to 1/2 pound cooked medium shrimp after you make your mac & cheese.

Cajun Shrimp Mac & Cheese: Add 1/3 to 1/2 pound shrimp and 1/4 teaspoon Cajun seasoning after you make your mac & cheese.

Beans and Tomatoes Mac & Cheese: Heat 1/2 cup diced tomatoes with juice and 1/2 cup and red, black or white beans (drained) in the microwave and add to the mac & cheese.

Fruit Mac & Cheese: Add some diced apple, pineapple, mandarin orange, mango or other fruit of choice. You can use canned pineapple, mandarin oranges, mangos and pears, just be sure to drain them first.

Now you can start cleaning out the fridge and pantry with these other great additions: black olives, roasted red peppers, chopped sun dried tomatoes in oil, chopped sautéed mushrooms, corn kernels, chopped kielbasa or cooked hot dogs (the kids will love it!),

Chopped cooked Italian sausage, chopped pepperoni or salami…I think you get the picture!

CHAPTER 26

AS AMERICAN AS MOM AND APPLE PIE

I love Mother's Day.

It's truly a holiday that celebrates the heroes of our age (or any age for that matter).

Not to take away anything from July 4th, Veterans Day and Memorial Day. I know that I would probably not be writing this if it weren't for the brave American men and women who paid the ultimate price for my freedom.

Heck, without them we all might've found ourselves working in a non-air conditioned plant for a dollar a month adding melamine and other toxins to baby formula for the health and economic well-being of The State.

Well...At least the males of The State since so many females, and yes, future moms, are aborted (for the good of The State, of course). Can you say, "Nice revolution you got started there, Chairman Mao."? Hmm...I knew you could.

So yes. I salute those great men and women - past and present - who guarantee our freedom.

But the truth of the matter is: most of us would not even be here if it weren't for moms.

"Wait," I hear some of you saying. "Don't you mean all of us wouldn't be here if it weren't for moms?"

Perhaps. Except that I have a few friends who, in spite of their loud cries of denial, have questionable pedigrees.

Don't believe me? Then you haven't met my friend Alan.

But back to moms.

Here's the deal: Moms put up with a lot.

Think about it.

Our moms cleaned up all the crap in our diapers when we were little ones. And most moms have been cleaning up our crap ever since. I know my Mom has.

When my Dad was murdered back in 1976, my Mom went on to start several successful businesses and helped put three of us through college. One of us went on to be an accountant. One a teacher. And one a dreamer.

I'll let you sort out who was who.

And even though she felt that I would've been a great lawyer, flying a desk just isn't in my genes - the genes that she herself and my Dad passed down to me (I couldn't picture either of them flying a desk).

No. Instead of flying a desk, I chose to fly by the seat of my pants. Which, incidentally, is not something one should list under "Applicable Skills" when typing up a résumé. Trust me on that one.

Anyway, my Mom has supported me both spiritually and financially throughout my years of successful self-employment and self-unemployment. I'm highly skilled at both. It's even on my résumé.

So here's to moms.

My first cookbook was dedicated to my wife. The next cookbook will go out to my Mom.

And if you don't have a book that you can dedicate to your mom, stop by and tell her you love her with some flowers and an apple pie.

I know she'll love it.

And if she's like my mom, she'll even offer to clean up the mess.

God bless moms!

• APPLE BROWN BETTY •

When I was growing up in New York, Apple Brown Betty was a staple in our high school cafeteria. The lunch ladies always made it from scratch. Here's a delicious version scaled down from 500 servings to 2.

PREP: 10 minutes   COOK: 1-1/2 hours

INGREDIENTS
  2 slices white bread, toasted
  1-1/2 cups cored, peeled and sliced tart apples
  1/4 cup white sugar
  1/4 cup brown sugar
  1/2 teaspoon ground cinnamon
  1/8 teaspoon ground cloves
  3 tablespoons melted unsalted butter
  Whipped cream (home-made, canned or frozen)

DIRECTIONS
  1. Grease a small casserole dish with unsalted butter.

  2. Tear toast into bite-size pieces and place in a greased casserole, then top with apples.

  3. Combine sugars and cinnamon; sprinkle over apples. Drizzle with butter.

  4. Cover and bake at 350° for 1 hour, stirring after 30 minutes.

Top with whipped cream and serve.

COOKING OUTSIDE THE LINES VARIATIONS

Substitute peaches, apricots, mangoes, or even pineapple for the apples. Delish!

CHAPTER 27

IF YOU CAN'T SAY SOMETHING NICE...

Someone once told me that if you can't say something nice about someone or something, then don't say anything at all.

I think that's good advice.

And it may just explain why all conversations stop and an eerie hush fills the room whenever I happen to enter.

But enough about me.

In this chapter I'll attempt to comment on a few topics. And if I can't say something nice, then you will have to endure the silence.

Bestselling Florida writers who are real people. I've had the privilege to meet and chat with a few great writers over the past couple of years. Sure, these guys hail from Florida, but they are no strangers to best-seller lists. Here's what impressed me: They were willing to chat with folks that loved their work. Why does that impress me? Because I've met other artists who couldn't give a rat's ass about the "little folk" who wanted to express their appreciation for the artist's work and how it added to their lives. Of course they overlook the fact that it's these "little folk" who buy the art that gives these snobs an opportunity to appear before the cameras and commence to snubbing the same "little folk" that put them there. So, here's a hat's off to Carl Hiaasen, Tim Dorsey and Randy Wayne White. Great writers who are also real people. I'm sure there are more; I just haven't met them yet.

Artists who despise their customers *<crickets chirping>*

Locally grown fruits and vegetables. By locally grown I'm talking about the produce you grow in your own backyard. Back in the day, when we had some real land, my wife planted a garden that produced wonderful tomatoes, squash, peppers, corn and watermelon. When we eventually moved to the inner city, we didn't have that option. Nor did we in the suburbs. The next best thing? Visiting local markets (and even good grocers) that offered something much like that she grew in our backyard.

Frozen veggies and fruits in sauce. *<crickets chirping>*

McDonalds' coffee. Okay, leaving aside all the concern about fast food and the ubiquitousness of this particular franchise, the fact is, McDonalds serves up some great Joe. I know, I know, there are legions of fans for the offerings of that ubiquitous coffee franchise from the Pacific northwest, but I for one, always thought their bitter and over-priced coffee tasted like...oops...I almost violated my principle. So...back to Mickey Dee's coffee. It's great and at a great price.

Gourmet coffee that's served with a shot of pretention. *<crickets chirping>*

Pasta dishes made from scratch. How easy can this be? Boil some noodles and add a simple homemade sauce (or yes, even from a jar or can). What will it take? 10 or 15 minutes? It fed generations and it fed them well. Here's to simple food!

Processed pasta dishes in a can. *<crickets chirping>*

Chicken Goujonettes. This is the original bite-sized chicken recipe created by the French. Real chicken breast fillets pounded and sliced into strips, a wholesome egg and butter coating, seasoned with spices, and dredged in breadcrumbs, then sautéed in oil (rather than deep fried). Great for lunch, dinner or a late-night snack.

Fast food chicken nuggets. *<crickets chirping>*

This is a start. I know I'll think of more. But again, enough about me. What inspires you to speak out? And what drives you to silence?

And while you're thinking about that, let's whip up some chicken to snack on.

• GOUJONETTES DE POULET •
(Chicken Nuggets)

PREP: 10 minutes   COOK: 15 minutes

INGREDIENTS

1 pound boneless, skinless chicken thighs or breasts, thinly sliced or cut into 1-inch chunks

1 egg, beaten

1 cup Italian breadcrumbs

1/4 cup grated Parmesan cheese

1/2 teaspoon Hungarian sweet paprika

1/2 teaspoon garlic powder

Kosher salt and freshly ground black pepper to taste

1/4 cup olive or canola oil

DIRECTIONS

1. In a shallow bowl, lightly beat egg. In another shallow bowl or zip lock bag, combine the breadcrumbs, cheese, paprika, and garlic powder. Season chicken with salt and pepper to taste.

2. Dip the chicken into the egg then dredge in the seasoned bread crumbs (or place into the bag and shake to coat).

3. Heat a 10-inch skillet over medium heat. Add olive oil and swirl to coat. Add chicken and sauté until lightly brown and tender, about 5 minutes.

4. Transfer chicken to a plate lined with paper towels with a slotted spoon to drain.

• SPICY OVEN FRIES •

PREP: 10 minutes   COOK: 40 minutes

INGREDIENTS
   2 large baking potatoes
   1 tablespoon olive oil
   1/2 teaspoon chili powder
   1/2 teaspoon cumin
   1/2 teaspoon Hungarian paprika
   1/2 teaspoon oregano
   1/4 teaspoon garlic powder
   1/8 teaspoon ground thyme
   Pinch cayenne pepper or more to taste.

DIRECTIONS:
   1.   Preheat oven to 450°.

   2.   Cut each potato into eight wedges. Combine the remaining ingredients in a
        medium bowl. Add potatoes and toss to coat.

   3.   Place potatoes on a baking sheet and bake for 20 minutes. Turn and cook for
        an additional 10 minutes or until potatoes are golden brown and crisp.

CHAPTER 28

WHY DOES MY PRODUCE DEPARTMENT THINK IT'S A RAIN FOREST?

I was talking to my friend, Jill, and she mentioned how irked she gets when her produce department pipes in the sound of thunder and rain over the loudspeakers whenever the misters are activated.

My local supermarket does the same. And now that she's mentioned it, that little ploy perturbs me as well. Particularly when I see some senior citizens scattering about, rushing to unfold their umbrellas and don their raincoats whenever the first clap of thunder roars over the PA system. I even saw one octogenarian, in an effort to keep her obviously just-styled hair from getting drenched, tear a plastic bag off the spool next to the green peppers and yank it down over her head.

Fortunately, I was there to yank it back off when she started turning blue.

Why do supermarkets do this? Is it to make us think that these veggies are so fresh even the rain followed them inside? Is it a ploy to keep us from picking up the produce and squeezing it? (After all, who wants to squeeze anything in a thunderstorm, unless of course you're trying to squeeze yourself into a bus stop filled with thirteen other people who got there first?) Or perhaps it's an attempt to engage all of our senses in the shopping experience - thus making it more pleasurable?

I think it's the latter. One popular Florida supermarket chain even claimed the tag line: "Where Shopping Is a Pleasure." They plastered this motto on the front of their stores, their shopping carts, and their bags. Even the nametags on the bag boys proclaimed it.

Now I don't know about you, but I can think of at least a half-dozen pleasurable experiences right off the top of my head, and grocery shopping is not one of them.

But I imagine that in their desire to make shopping as pleasurable as, say, dining on a delicious gourmet meal, savoring a fine single malt scotch, or having wild unbridled sex with your soul mate, supermarkets have chosen to engage all of our senses with the sounds of rumbling thunder and misty rain.

Of course, my question is: Why stop at the produce department? Why not have clucking poultry and the pungent smell of chicken poop piped in at the meat department? Or the smell of wet hay and cow manure in the dairy department? And think of how your bread-buying experience would be enhanced if all of the ladies behind the bakery counter were all pleasantly plump, sported cheeks the color of rose petals, and spoke in a dialect that could only be described as rural Sicilian?

And how about the deli department? Imagine how authentic it would be if they piped in the sound of old lady Sussman berating the poor slob behind the counter because her order of sliced pastrami was 1/8 of an ounce off? Oh, wait; old lady Sussman already does that on a regular basis in my store. Never mind.

Hmm, now that I've thought some more about it, I'm convinced that the reason they pipe in the rain forest sound track is to engage all of our senses: to make a mundane, weekly chore, a pleasure.

And in a way it worked. I now count grocery shopping as a highly pleasurable experience, just a notch below dining on a delicious gourmet meal, savoring a fine single malt Scotch, or having wild unbridled sex with my soul mate. And also a notch below petting the dog, binge watching Netflix, and scratching an itch when no one is looking.

So here's to the pleasures of shopping. May all of us find within it a 'happy ending'. But only when no one is looking.

• ROASTED VEGETABLES FOUR WAYS •

Here's a delicious dish to launch into after a quick visit to your local farmers' market. It's a great way to serve up veggies and it's also very versatile. I recommend potatoes, onions, carrots, peppers, summer squash and mushrooms, but feel free to improvise by adding or substituting eggplant, parsnips, asparagus, winter squash, etc. I've also included four dressings but I'm sure you will think of some more. There's really no "wrong" way to make this so have at it!

PREP: 15 minutes   COOK: 1 hour

INGREDIENTS
  2 potatoes cut into 1-inch cubes

  1 sweet potato cut into 1-inch cubes

  1 small rutabaga cut into 1-inch cubes

  2 carrots, peeled and cut into 1-inch cubes

  1 large onion cut into wedges

  1/4 pound mushrooms, cut in half

  1 medium zucchini or yellow squash cut into 1-inch cubes

  2 red bell peppers cut into 1-inch cubes

DIRECTIONS
  1. Preheat oven to 425°.

  2. Bring a pot of water to a boil over high heat. Parboil potatoes, rutabaga and carrots for 2 minutes. Drain well.

  3. In a large bowl, combine the potatoes, rutabaga, carrots, onions, mushrooms, zucchini and bell peppers. Whisk dressing ingredients (see below) in a small bowl and pour over vegetables and toss.

  4. Place vegetables in a single layer in a baking dish and roast for 45 minutes, stirring every 10 or 15 minutes until tender.

Serve over orzo or other small pasta.

• ITALIAN STYLE DRESSING •

INGREDIENTS
    1-1/2 tablespoons olive oil

    1/4 cup fresh lemon juice

    6 cloves garlic, pressed or minced

    3 teaspoons dried rosemary, crushed

    2 teaspoons dried oregano

    1 teaspoon kosher salt

• MIDDLE EASTERN DRESSING •

INGREDIENTS
    3 tablespoons olive oil

    1-1/2 tablespoons lemon juice

    1 tablespoon white wine vinegar

    1/2 teaspoon cumin

    1/4 teaspoon black pepper

    Pinch of kosher salt to taste

    3 cloves garlic, crushed

• CARIBBEAN DRESSING •

INGREDIENTS

3 tablespoons soy sauce

1 tablespoon olive oil

2 tablespoons red wine vinegar

1 tablespoon brown sugar

1 small onion, chopped

1/2 teaspoon ground cinnamon

1/2 teaspoon ground cloves

1/4 teaspoon ground nutmeg

1/2 teaspoon ground black pepper

1/2 teaspoon dried thyme

2 teaspoons grated fresh ginger root

1 clove garlic, pressed or minced

1 fresh jalapeno pepper, chopped (seeds and ribs removed for milder heat)

• ORIENTAL DRESSING •

INGREDIENTS

1/3 cup soy sauce

1/3 cup rice wine vinegar

1 tablespoon grated fresh ginger root

1 tablespoon honey

1 tablespoon sesame oil

3 cloves garlic, crushed or minced

1/2 teaspoon ground anise seed

MEMORIAL DAY WEEKEND – THREE FULL DAYS TO PROVE THAT MOST OF US CAN'T COOK OUTDOORS

To me, there's no better way to kick off the summer than to have a national three-day holiday. And there's no better way to show that most of us can't cook outdoors than to give us three full days to prove it.

You noticed I said "us."

That's because for quite a while, I was one of those who couldn't cook outdoors. Now don't get me wrong. I could start a fire and hurl something on it. But it wasn't really what I would now call "cooking." It was more like "cremation." I'm sure I'm not the first backyard cook to have been cited by the sheriff for abusing an animal corpse during a cookout.

And do you know what was really sad? I didn't even know I couldn't cook outdoors.

I mean, how hard could it be? Just start up a raging fire in the old kettle grill and toss on a hunk of raw meat. Cook it for a beer or two, then yank it off, hack at it 'til it resembled servings, and slather it with a bucket or two of bar-b-q sauce. Then call everyone to the table and serve it with the canned baked beans the wife re-heated, the potato salad that Aunt Minnie brought (geez, I hope she kept it in the fridge this year), the chips and dip that John and Julie from next door brought, and, of course, the two bags of ice that cheapskate Uncle Willy brings every year to keep the beer that everyone else bought cold.

So what's not to like?

Besides the food and Uncle Willy? Nothing.

Like many of us who cook outdoors, I had no reference point. That is, until I met Eddie and Michael. These two friends aren't related, but you'll often find them at the same cookouts. Eddie does the chicken, fish and other assorted seafood. Michael handles the beef and pork. They both excel at grilling veggies.

The first time I saw them in action and tasted the items that came off the grill I wanted to be them. But when my wife looked over at me from across the picnic table in a near-swoon as she sampled the beef and shrimp hot off Eddie and Michael's grill and sighed, "Why can't you grill like Eddie and Michael?" I knew the gauntlet had been thrown down.

So I made it a point to study these two men until I could match their technique and glorious results. It took a couple of years, but here's what I learned:

Don't be a Tightwad. Spring for Some Good Food.

As a rule, I've always bought good cuts of meat and fish whenever I planned on cooking indoors. But outside? What's the point if I'm only going to char it to hell? Why spend $20 a pound on a filet-of-something when I could buy a hunk of backyard-something for $3 a pound? It made complete sense until I tasted Eddie's salmon steaks with lemon butter and Michael's filet mignon with a glacé to die for.

Now, I have to say this, Michael manages one of the top restaurants in the city so he is able to get the really primo cuts of meat that I could never hope to buy. Eddie? He's a regular guy like me, but he buys his cookout entrees from the butcher and the seafood market, so I had no excuse. Right then, I made a vow to never buy my meat and seafood in large opaque packages from the "Must Sell Today by Five" bin of my grocery store again. That decision in and of itself made a huge difference. Plus, I see that club stores like Costco and Sam's are carrying more Prime cuts of beef. If you're a member, pick some up. The few extra dollars per pound is well worth it to get beef that was once only available to high-end restaurants.

Use the Right Tools.

You can spend a fortune on specialty grilling gear at your local big box hardware store or gourmet shop but it's not really necessary. Apart from investing in a good grill (I still use my old school Weber and there are many great affordable gas grills on the market; just do your research via Consumer Reports or Cooks Illustrated) there are only a few tools you really need:

- Chimney starter
- Spring loaded tongs (I use mine from the kitchen)
- Wide spatula – one that's offset for easier turning
- Basting brush – Skip the kitchen store and pick up some cheap paint brushes at Home Depot or Loews and use them for sauce. Toss them when they get too gunky after washing.
- Spray water bottle for flare-ups
- Wire grill basket for fish and delicate veggies
- Flat stainless steel skewers (of bamboo skewers)
- Wire brush to clean grill (Again, I head to the paint department at Home Depot. The wire brush they sell is a lot cheaper than specialty grill brushes)

That's pretty much it.

Oh, one more thing. If you use natural charcoal chunks instead of briquettes, you'll find that some of the pieces can slip between the bottom grate of your grill. I invested in a second bottom grate then lay it perpendicular on top of the other grate. That way, small chunks of charcoal stay where they're supposed to.

Cook on a Clean Grill.
Many of us pride ourselves on the layers of black gunk that years of outdoor cooking have created on our grills. We believe that this accumulation not only adds subtle flavor to our food, but the layers of grime and blackened fat draw off all of the impurities in the food we're grilling. Boy, were we wrong. When I had a piece of jumbo grilled shrimp fresh off Eddie's grill and did not detect even a hint of the baby back ribs I cooked last weekend? I was sold. So now I clean my grill either after I'm done cooking while whatever I cooked rests (see below) or if I'm in a hurry, I'll brush it the next time after the grate heats up.

Make sure grate is hot! Charcoal: at least 5 minutes. Gas: 15 minutes.
Do you find that most of the meat, poultry, fish or veggies continually stick to your grate? It's a common problem. But it can be rectified by doing two things. Make sure your grate is hot before putting any food on it. Charcoal will take at least 15 minutes and gas might take up to 15 minutes. The second step is to:

Oil the Grate Just Before Adding the Food.
If you really don't enjoy peeling the food off of your grill with a putty knife to serve to your guests, you'll need to oil it just before you add your food. There are several spray can products on the market but I avoid anything that's aerosol near an open flame. I just pour some vegetable oil in a small bowl, wad up a paper towel, the dip it in the oil with my tongs and oil the grate. You don't want to do this until your ready to add the food. If you do it too early, the oil will vaporize and won't be effective.

If You Cook at Night, Use a Light.
When I watched Eddie and Michael whip up some late night surf and turf I was surprised that they did so with the outdoor spotlights on. I had always thought that the true and most iconic way to grill outdoors was in whatever light the twinkling stars and glowing moon could give you. Either that or a flashlight. The smaller the better so as not to ruin the overall ambiance. Once again, I was wrong. When I turned on the porch light I was amazed at how much control I had over whatever items I had on the grill. I mean, they were not backlit by the roaring flames in the kettle where everything, regardless of how rare or well done they were, all resembled solid black lumps on the grate.

Pay Attention.
The last important lesson I learned from these two grill men was their penchant for paying attention to whatever they had on the grill. By doing so, they knew when to turn each item, when to move them to cooler parts of the grill, and when to remove them for serving. Sure, it may be much more fun to throw something on the grill and then join everyone else in the limbo dance by the pool, but your steaks, shrimp

and chicken breasts will taste much better after a few minutes on the grill rather than the time it takes for everyone to prove to everyone else that now that the limbo pole is a mere 18-inches from the ground they can still make it under, even after six consecutive (unsuccessful) tries.

Let grilled food rest for at least 5 minutes.
This is another tip that's often neglected. But if you want juicier steak, pork, chicken or even fish, let it rest for a few minutes to allow the juices to redistribute themselves throughout the meat.

Brush the grate when you're done.
I'm sorry to have to repeat myself, but while the food is resting, take that wire brush and clean the grate while it's still hot. You and your guests at the next cookout will appreciate it!

I hope these tips will revolutionize your outdoor cooking experience. In chapter 32, I share some tips about 'grilling' indoors. Until then, I need to send Uncle Willy out for out for another couple of bags of ice. We're gonna whip up some serious margaritas.

CHAPTER 30

DARK DAYS, STEAK FAJITAS, AND THE DAMAGE AND THE DUST

Have you ever had one of "those" days?

I'm not talking about one of those days when the woman behind the counter at the DMV stares at you as if she had suddenly forgotten English. Or one of those days when the soufflé you labored over for hours resembles a piece of damp cardboard. Or one of those days when your teacher tells you to get up in front of the class so you can give the oral report that she forgot to tell you about. (Or even worse, when your teacher tells you to give the report and you realize you're naked.)

No. I'm talking about one of those really bad days. The kind of day when you wake up and the gray sky outside your window threatens to crush you like a heavy stone. When you cast off the covers and find yourself buried beneath the damage and the dust.

Or maybe it's not one of those "days". But one of those weeks. Or months. Or years.

This is beyond an English language memory loss, a collapsed soufflé, or a naked recitation in front of the whole class.

We're talking about serious stuff. Lost cell phone? Runny eggs? Dead car battery? Forgotten anniversary? Heck. Mere child's play.

Have you been there? I have. Why just this past Sunday I was there. Loved one. Stricken. Emergency room. A gazillion medical tests. Touch and go. Yep. Lots of damage. Lots of dust.

So I found myself trying to make sense of it all, knees struggling to bend in prayer, drowning my sorrows in a couple of Blue Moons, a bowl of orange slices, and a Green Bay Packers game on the big screen. I even had a pound and a half of flat iron steak marinating in some Key lime juice and cumin to make a pile of fajitas that only someone who was not in my state could enjoy. But alas, I'd lost my appetite.

Then our two dogs started barking out on the porch like there was no tomorrow. I glanced through the blinds and saw my friend John Mark down in the driveway waving like a grounds crewman trying to guide a wayward 747 into the gate during a blizzard. I jumped up and wrangled the dogs inside so John Mark could make his way up the porch stairs unscathed and with calves intact.

I threw open the door and John Mark strode into our living room with a smile that lit up the entire space. We embraced and exchanged greetings while my wife poured him something to drink. I turned off the TV and flicked on the stereo. Peter Himmelman's rollicking song "Damage and the Dust" spilled from the speakers. Energized, I bounded into the kitchen, grilled the flat iron, sautéed the onions and peppers, and then wrapped them all up in warm tortillas. We poured some red wine and feasted on this thrown-together meal as if it were prepared for kings. We laughed and spoke of memories that surely brought smiles to the angels. Seriously, we laughed so hard we all dripped salsa on our jeans and spilled wine on our shirts.

Two hours and many stories later, John Mark climbed into his minivan and headed north leaving my spirit a tad bit lighter and my shirt stained with the memory of good company.

John Mark's laughter and joy scraped away some of the damage and dust from me that night and I went to bed realizing that I have the opportunity to help at least one person every day. Who knows what a kind word could mean to the haggard cashier at the grocery store. The dollar to the homeless guy with the misspelled sign on the corner. Asking the elderly man or woman in the pew next to me for advice. Or how that soufflé, imperfect as it might be, may satisfy those who are gathered around my table.

Yep. Who knows? Our small acts of kindness, even the meals we prepare, might heal some of the damage that others bear.

Heck, and those acts of kindness just might remove some of the dust that covers us.

It did me.

Now, how about some more of those steak fajitas?

• STEAK FAJITAS WITH A SPIN •

This cooking method may be a little different than you're used to. But trust me, it rocks.

PREP: 5 minutes   MARINATE: 2+ hours
COOK: 15 minutes

INGREDIENTS

3/4 pound flat iron steak

1 tablespoon chili powder

1/2 teaspoon dried oregano

1/2 teaspoon ground cumin

1/2 teaspoon cayenne pepper
(more or less to taste)

1 small onion, sliced thin

2 cloves garlic, crushed

1/2 cup fresh key lime juice (or bottled Nelly & Joe's is fine)

1 medium onion, sliced

1 red or green pepper, sliced

4 tortillas, warmed

Grated cheese and salsa or other condiments

DIRECTIONS

1. Combine the chili powder, oregano, cumin and cayenne pepper in a small bowl, then rub the mixture into the steak. Place the steak in a re-sealable plastic bag and add the onions and garlic to distribute. Pour in the lime juice and marinate in the fridge for at least 2 hours.

2. When the steak is nearly done marinating, preheat your oven as high as it'll go (500°or higher). Place a cast iron skillet on the stove and heat over medium-high heat until it becomes very hot and turns grey (10 minutes or so).

3. Remove the steak from the bag and pat dry. Place the steak into the cast iron skillet then immediately place the skillet on the bottom of the pre-heated oven. (If you can't place it right on the floor of the oven, place it on the lowest rack). Cook for 3 minutes. Turn the steak and cook for an additional 3 minutes for medium-rare.

4. While the steak is cooking, sauté the onion and pepper in a lightly oiled skillet until slightly tender.

5. Remove steak and let sit for at least 5 minutes. Wrap the tortillas in a damp paper towel and nuke for 1 minute). Slice the steak very thin across the grain and serve on warm tortillas with the sautéed onions, peppers and condiments.

Serve with some cold sangria or a couple of Blue Moons.

CHAPTER 31

IF TODAY IS FATHER'S DAY, WHY HAVE PEOPLE BEEN CALLING ME A MOTHER ALL WEEK?

I'm glad fathers have a special day of their own because we have it pretty rough these days. Especially when it comes to television. Just look at how dads have been portrayed over the past ten years or so: Red Forman, Homer Simpson, Tony Soprano, Peter Griffin...

Wow, I'm thinking of getting a sex change operation just thinking about these TV icons and the fact that we share two things in common: we're all male and we're all dads.

Of course many of us pine for the good old days of Ward Cleaver, Danny Thomas and Andy Taylor. Heck, even those in the not-too-distant past were worthy of emulation: Howard Cunningham, Cliff Huxtable and Carl Winslow...

So when did it become open season on dads? When did the word "dad" find its way into Roget's thesaurus as a synonym of "jackass"?

Here's my theory.

"*They*" did it. And by that I mean the mysterious and elusive "*they*" that are the cause of most of society's problems. Although we've never met them in person, we quote them all the time as in: "*They* say that (fill in the blank) is the cause of all (fill in the blank.)"

So until I find out exactly who '"*they*" are, I guess I'll just have to suck it up until someone in TV land decides to stop making dads look like the south end of a northward headed donkey.

But to be honest, I can't blame it entirely on "*they.*"

I think we dads brought some of it on ourselves.

Think about it for a minute.

How many times have we asked our kids rhetorical questions that, if they answered them correctly, would not have boded well for either of us? I'm thinking about the questions every dad asks that shouldn't be answered. Questions like:

How many times have I told you not to do that? (Possible kid answer: Eleven).

Or -

"Do you want me to take off my belt?" (Possible kid answer: Only if the neighbors get a kick out of seeing the boxers we got you last Father's Day).

Or -

What do I look like, an idiot? (Possible kid answer: Well, now that you mention it, Dad, when you wear your plaid shorts with that Gators t-shirt you do look kinda like an…)

And speaking of goofy outfits. Why do so many of us insist on wearing them when we decide to grill outside?

Or better yet, why do so many of us who have never set foot in a kitchen (unless it's to grab a beer out of the fridge or dip a spoon into whatever the wife has simmering on the stove) assume that we can cook outdoors where temperamental flames, unpredictable wind, stifling heat, fluctuant barometric pressure and the sight of that tanned and nubile next door neighbor in the size-2 bikini sunning herself by the pool can wreak havoc on our culinary endeavors?

I'll tell you why.

Because men like fire and men like to burn things.

I'm serious.

In a recent study by the National Conference of Those Who Study Such Things, male arsonists were shown to outnumber female arsonists by a margin of 6 to 1. The only other categories where males outshine their female counterparts? Misplacing the remote control (10 to 1), refusing to ask for directions when lost (97 to 1) and scratching their own crotch (when the numbers jump to a mind-boggling 13,478 to 1).

So yes. Give us dads a Weber grill, a 25-pound bag of charcoal, a quart of lighter fluid, a hunk of meat, and a couple of six-packs in the fridge and we will occupy ourselves for the better part of the afternoon. Let us invite some pals over and we'll make a whole day of it.

Then we'll knock back some beers, suck in our stomachs (to impress Ms. Tanned and Nubile next door) and compliment one another on the killer fire we've created while we scratch our crotches and watch the wives run for the fire extinguisher.

Man, I think I'm digging the hole deeper here. I'd better stop before I get myself into more trouble.

I mean, what do I look like, an idiot?

Don't answer that.

• BEST FRIGGIN' BRAT RECIPE EVER •

At one time I figured brats were easy to make. Heck, they're just hot dogs on steroids, right? So all you need to do is rip open the package, hurl those babies onto the grill, and cook 'em just short of incineration. Simple as that!

Boy was I wrong.

In order to learn how to cook brats right I had to go to the source: Wisconsin. Milwaukee to be exact. Because the Poles who settled there know their brats like we Irish know our whiskey.

I got this recipe from Krzysztof Dworaczyk, a burly guy with a wooden leg and glass eye, who ran a brat stand down in Lincoln Village. I didn't have much money on me so I asked if he would be willing to trade a brat or two for some vowels.

He was more than willing.

And let me tell you, it rocks. You will never go back to plain old hot dogs again.

PREP: 10 minutes   COOK: 1 hour

INGREDIENTS
  4 good brats. (If you can get them from your butcher, great. If not, Johnsonville is a good national brand).
  1/4 cup (1/2 stick) unsalted butter, divided
  1 large Spanish or sweet onion (Vidalia) sliced
  3 garlic cloves, minced or crushed
  1/2 teaspoon kosher salt
  2 cans (or bottles) of full-bodied amber beer - none of that "lite" crap
  4 brat buns

DIRECTIONS

1. Preheat outdoor grill.

2. Melt 3 tablespoons unsalted butter in a Dutch oven over medium-high heat. Add 1/4 of the onion and sauté until soft and translucent, about 8 minutes. Add garlic and sauté an addition 2 minutes. Add the brats, salt and beer and bring to a slow boil.

3. Quickly lower heat and simmer for 30 minutes. Remove from heat and let sit, covered.

4. In the meantime, heat remaining butter in a 10-inch skillet over medium-high heat. Add remaining onion slices and sauté until soft and translucent, about 8 minutes.

5. Remove brats from pot and grill over medium heat until nicely brown, about 10 - 15 minutes.

6. Serve on buns with sautéed onions and plenty of good beer.

• CREAMY COLE SLAW •

This is creamy coleslaw, not the drier and crunchier version. I think it works well with brats.

PREP: 10 minutes   CHILL: 2+ hours

INGREDIENTS
  1 (16-ounce) bag coleslaw mix
  1/2 small onion, minced (optional)
  2/3 cup mayonnaise
  2 tablespoons sugar
  3 tablespoons milk
  2 tablespoons rice or white wine vinegar
  2 teaspoons kosher salt
  1/4 teaspoon pepper

DIRECTIONS
  1.   Combine all ingredients except coleslaw mix and onion in a large bowl.

  2.   Add the coleslaw and onion and toss to coat.

  3.   Cover and refrigerate for at least 2 hours to allow flavors to meld.

Serves 4 - 6

• TRADTIONAL POTATO SALAD •

Looks like a lot of ingredients, but once you prepare the potatoes and chop the onion and celery, it comes together quickly with stuff you have in your cupboard and fridge.

PREP: 10 minutes   COOK: 30 minutes
CHILL: 2+ hours

INGREDIENTS
  2 pounds russet potatoes (3 or 4 medium), peeled and cut into 3/4-inch cubes

  1 tablespoon salt

  2 tablespoons distilled white vinegar or apple cider vinegar

  1 medium rib celery, chopped fine (about 1/2 cup)

  2 tablespoons minced red onion

  3 tablespoons sweet pickle relish

  1/2 cup mayonnaise (or more if salad is too dry for your taste – you can add more after you pull it all together)

  3/4 teaspoon powdered mustard

  3/4 teaspoon celery seed

  2 tablespoons minced fresh parsley leaves

  1/4 teaspoon ground black pepper

  2 large hard-cooked eggs, peeled and cut into 1/4-inch cubes (optional)

DIRECTIONS
  1. Place potatoes in large saucepan and add water to cover by 1 inch. Bring to boil over medium-high heat; add 1 tablespoon salt, reduce heat to medium, and simmer, stirring once or twice, until potatoes are tender, about 8 minutes.

  2. Drain potatoes and transfer to large bowl. Add vinegar and, using rubber spatula, toss gently to combine. Let stand until potatoes are just warm, about 20 minutes.

  3. Meanwhile, in small bowl, stir together celery, onion, pickle relish, mayonnaise, mustard powder, celery seed, parsley, pepper, and 1/2 teaspoon salt. Using rubber spatula, gently fold dressing and eggs, if using, into potatoes. Cover with plastic wrap and refrigerate until chilled, about 1 hour; serve. (Potato salad can be covered and refrigerated for up to 1 day.)

CHAPTER 32

IT'S RAINING, IT'S POURING, THE OLD MAN IS...A LITTLE TICKED OFF 'CUZ HE WANTED TO GRILL OUT THIS WEEKEND

So you bought a slab of ribs, some chicken legs, or some mighty fine ribeye steaks to throw on the grill this weekend. But it's raining cats and dogs outside. Don't despair!

Last weekend I was going grill out but it'd been raining non-stop for the two weeks with no sign of letting up. I know this has probably happened to you, too. So here are some perfect recipes for creating mouth-watering ribs, chicken or steak indoors.

If fact, these are so good you may want to make them indoors even when it's not raining.

RIBS

First, start off with the right ribs. I opt for St. Louis-style ribs because they're meatier than their baby back cousins and are easier to separate than regular ribs (because they've had the sternum bone, cartilage, and rib tips removed). However, do make them with baby backs, decrease cooking time by about 1/2 hour to the cooking time. If using regular spare rib ribs, add about 1/2 hour.

Fortunately, St. Louis ribs were on sale that weekend for $1.99 a pound at my local grocery store, and Sweet Baby Ray's Bar-B-Q Sauce®, was BOGO. Needless to say, I stocked up.

Here are a couple of hints before beginning: Make sure you have on hand large heavy-duty aluminum foil, that way when you wrap the ribs, you'll only have one seam running lengthwise across the top. And by the way, don't you hate it when your roll of foil (or plastic wrap or wax paper) falls out of the box when you pull on it? I do. That's why you need to check the ends of the box. Most brands have a small cutout that you can push in to hold the tube in place when you pull on it. I've been cooking for decades and just found this out!

Also, even though some recipes specify whether you should place the ribs on either the shiny or dull side of the foil, the fact is that it doesn't matter with regular aluminum foil; the two sheens are part of the manufacturing process and won't affect your cooking at all.

Some recipes also suggest you rinse the ribs off in the sink and then pat them dry. I don't recommend you rinse any pork (or chicken, for that matter) in the sink before patting dry because you're likely to do more harm than reap any benefit from rinsing meat or poultry. Here's why: when you rinse raw pork or chicken, you're splattering juices all over the sink surface, faucet handle and surrounding countertops. Unless you diligently clean your surroundings with soap and hot water right after rinsing, you run a high risk of contamination on these surfaces. Besides, there's nothing that you'll be rinsing off from your pork or chicken that won't be taken care of by cooking. So just remove the pork or chicken from the package, pat dry, and proceed.

I also suggest making your own rub because the main ingredient in most grocery store rubs is salt. (One brand I found that doesn't is Weber Dry Smoking Rub®.) Plus, making your own is sooo much cheaper. That being said, you'll be making more rub than you'll need for this recipe. But that's okay. Save whatever's left in an empty jar and use it on fish, chicken (see the chicken recipe below), home fries, scrambled eggs, top-sirloin or filet mignon, pork chops or pork loin – it'll really liven things up. (That's why I always double or triple the recipe)

CHICKEN

I recommend using bone-in chicken for these recipes. They will come out juicier.

When you're ready to make the chicken, remove it from the package and remove any large pieces of fat. Don't bother washing the chicken; you'll wind up doing more harm than good. There are no germs or bacteria on the chicken that won't be dealt with by cooking. However, washing raw chicken (or turkey or duck) in your sink will just spread any bacteria in the raw chicken juice onto your sink, nearby countertop, and faucet. Then you'll have to wash everything down with a bleach solution. It's better to just pat the pieces dry with a paper towel and proceed.

If you're using a rub, gently slip your fingers under the skin to loosen it from the meat (be careful not to tear the skin) then rub some of the spices underneath the skin. This will ensure that not only the skin, but the meat itself is seasoned. Plus, it'll be great for those who like to remove the skin before eating because they won't be removing all the rub when they ditch the skin.

BEEF

Face it, good grilling requires good beef. This is not the time to cut corners by purchasing beef cuts that won't be tender regardless of how you prepare or cook them. So, spring for beef that will reward you and your guests with both tenderness and flavor. Here are my recommendations: ribeye, NY strip, T-bone, and porterhouse. These cuts are the most traditional for grilling. However, you can also get good results from flat iron and top sirloin steaks. Skirt and flank steak are also good if you thinly slice them across the grain after grilling. Filet mignon is a popular cut but to me it's overrated in relation to its price because, while the cut is tender, it doesn't have much flavor (which is why you see it wrapped in bacon or served with a sauce).

• PERFECT RAINY DAY BAR-B-Q RIBS •
(Can be doubled for more servings)

PREP: 10 minutes   MARINATE: 1/2 hour or more
COOK: 2 hours, 45 minutes

INGREDIENTS

FOR THE RIBS:

1 rack St. Louis style pork ribs (about 3 lbs +/-)

1 bottle barbecue sauce (I like Sweet Baby Ray's Barbecue Sauce®)

A few drops of Liquid Smoke® (optional)

FOR THE RUB:

1/4 cup brown sugar

1-1/2 teaspoons garlic powder

1-1/2 teaspoons onion powder

1/2 teaspoon salt

1-1/2 teaspoons chili powder

1 teaspoon cumin

1 tablespoon smoked paprika

1/2 teaspoon cayenne pepper (or more depending on taste)

DIRECTIONS

1. Preheat the oven to 275°.

2. In a small bowl, mix dry rub ingredients until well combined.

3. Pat the ribs dry with paper towels and place on a piece of large, heavy-duty aluminum foil.

4. Remove the membrane from the back of the ribs. It's not a game-changer, but it does help the ribs absorb more rub. Here's how: Slip a butter knife beneath the membrane at the narrow end of the ribs and loosen. Grab the membrane with a paper towel (otherwise it will slip from your fingers) and peel it away from the ribs. Sometime you can do this in one fell swoop, but more often you'll have to do it in stages, as the membrane tends to tear.

5. Spread about 2 tablespoons dry rub on each side of the ribs (you can use more, just don't overdo it; you still want to taste the ribs!).

6. Wrap the foil tightly around the ribs place seam side up on a baking sheet. Let sit for 1/2 hour or more if desired (if resting for more than 1/2 hour, refrigerate).

7. Bake for on the upper-middle rack 2-1/2 hours until fork tender. If not fork tender after that time, return the ribs to oven and continue cooking, checking every 10 minutes, until the ribs are fork tender. (Why this might be so: perhaps your oven is not calibrated correctly. Some ovens may be off by 10 or 15 degrees! Best to buy a good oven thermometer so you get an accurate reading and adjust your oven temp accordingly).

8. Remove the ribs from the oven and turn the oven to broil. Move the rack to the top position.

9. Open the foil and carefully drain the liquid from the ribs. Stir the Liquid Smoke into the bar-b-q sauce if desired. Brush the barbecue sauce on the ribs, broil for about 3 minutes (Be careful not to let the sauce burn). Turn and brush some sauce over the other side and broil for 3 additional minutes.

10. Remove the ribs from the oven and rest 5 - 10 minutes before cutting. Serves 2 hungry diners with some leftovers.

• PERFECT RAINY DAY BAR-B-Q CHICKEN •

PREP: 5 minutes   MARINATE: 30+ minutes
COOK: 40 minutes

INGREDIENTS
  2 bone-in, skin-on chicken legs and 2 chicken thighs
  1 tablespoon dry rub (see Ribs Recipe above)
  1/2 cup barbecue sauce
  A few drops of Liquid Smoke (optional)

DIRECTIONS
1. Gently slide your fingers under the skin of the chicken to loosen it. Spread
    the rub underneath the skin being careful not to tear it. Place the chicken
    on a plate and baste with barbecue sauce. (If you're using Liquid Smoke,
    stir it into the barbecue sauce before basting.) Cover chicken with plastic
    wrap and marinate for at least 30 minutes in the refrigerator. The longer
    they sit, the better.

2. Turn the oven to broil and place the rack under the broiler. Line a rimmed
    baking sheet or broiler pan with aluminum foil (it will speed clean-up) and set
    a lightly-oiled cooking or cooling rack (like one used for baking) inside the
    baking sheet. While doing this is not a game-changer (you can just place the
    chicken a lightly-oiled broiler pan) but placing it on a rack will help ensure
    crispier skin.

3. Place the chicken on the rack in the baking sheet and broil until the sauce
    begins to brown, about 5 minutes. Turn the chicken and broil for an additional
    5 minutes.

4. Reduce the oven to 350° and move the rack to the middle of the oven. Brush
    the chicken with some more sauce and continue to cook for 15 minutes.
    Turn the chicken, brush with more sauce, and continue baking until chicken
    reaches 160° about 15 minutes longer. Remove chicken and let rest for 5
    minutes. Serve with additional sauce.

• PERFECT RAINY DAY STEAK •

Pan-searing steak is the ultimate way to prepare steak indoors. However, if you don't have a really good hood fan that vents to the outside, you'll find your smoke alarms coming to life while your guests run, gasping for air, to the nearest door or window. So here's an excellent way to get a savory, charred steak without filling your house full of smoke.

I suggest using boneless cuts for this recipe. Here's why: if you use a cut with the bone-in, the meat will shrink a bit during cooking (the bone will not) and will lose contact with the hot pan, thus robbing the meat of that wonderful flavor that a good sear provides. So save your t-bones, porterhouses, and bone-in ribeyes for the grill. Your taste buds will thank you.

PREP: Less than 5 minutes   REST: 1 hour
COOK: 10 minutes

INGREDIENTS
2 boneless ribeye or NY strip steaks   2 pats butter
Kosher salt and cracked ground pepper

DIRECTIONS
1. Remove the steaks from the refrigerator at least 45 minutes before cooking. Pat dry with paper towels and sprinkle liberally with kosher salt and cracked pepper. Press the pepper into the meat with the palm of your hand and let sit for 45 minutes. If you want to let them rest longer, return the steaks to the fridge.

2. Preheat your oven to its highest setting (at least 500°) and place an oven rack in its lowest position (Because I have gas, I remove the rack altogether because I can set my skillet right on the oven floor).

3. Preheat a cast iron skillet in the oven or over medium-high heat on your stove for 5 – 10 minutes until the bottom begins to turn grey and the pan begins to smoke. Don't use an aluminum or non-stick skillet for this. You'll ruin the pan.

4. Pat the steaks dry and lightly brush each side with canola oil. Add the steaks to the pan and immediately transfer the skillet to the oven. Roast the steaks for 3 minutes then turn and continue cooking an additional 2 or 3 minutes for medium rare.

5. Remove the steaks to a warm plate and top with a pat of butter. Lightly cover and allow to rest for 5 - 10 minutes (depending on how thick they are) so the juices redistribute themselves throughout the steak.

CHAPTER 33

A WORD ABOUT SALTING, SEARING, AND RESTING

Ask 3 chefs when it's best to salt steak and you might get 3 answers. Can science help? Absolute! The optimum time to salt your steak is at least 45 minutes before you plan to cook it. Here's why:

1. After a few minutes of salting your steak, juice will start to bead up on the surface. This is not good for searing purposes since the juice will form a barrier between the meat and the pan. You'll waste time and energy because you'll just wind up steaming the meat.

2. After 10 or 15 minutes, the juice that has pooled on the surface will form a brine that begins to break down the outer muscle structure of the steak allowing the meat to become more absorptive.

3. After 45 minutes, most of the juices have been reabsorbed through reverse osmosis, thus making the meat more tender and flavorful.

Searing

I've heard it. You've heard it. One must sear steaks to seal in the juices. Sounds good, but is it true? Unfortunately no. A steak will lose the same amount of juice whether you sear it or don't. So why sear? Because searing creates what's known as the Maillard Reaction. As the meat sears, a rich, caramelized crust that is loaded with flavor will develop on the outside of the steak.

Resting

Do you remember the last time you cut into a ribeye steak hot off the grill? Do you remember how your plate filled up with a pool of glorious steak juice? I do. That's not a good thing. If you allow your steak to rest for at least 5 minutes you'll not only avoid plateful of juice, but your steak will taste much better as well.

Here's why: as the steak begins to sear, the juices are forced towards the center, thus increasing a concentration of moisture in the middle of the steak. When you flip the steak over, the juices on that side of the steak are also forced to the center. Now the center is saturated with more liquid than it can fully absorb, so when you begin to slice it, those juices run out onto your plate. By letting the steak rest for 5 minutes, those juices will be redistributed throughout the entire steak. Now we're talking a seriously juicy steak.

CHAPTER 34

BUCKET LISTS AND PAPER CUTS

In a previous chapter, I mentioned that visiting Ireland was on my Bucket List. And in doing so, I was prompted to go back and take a look at the whole list. To be honest, I was quite encouraged with my progress, particularly since I've always tried to cast my cares to the wind and live my life to the fullest; To not only 'push the edge of the envelope' but to lick the flap in such a way that it might induce paper cuts on my tongue.

So I thought I'd share my list with you in hopes that it'll encourage you to reach for the stars as well. And because I love to cook, you'll see that many of them are food related. But I also love to sing, play instruments, and act the fool, so some of those are on there as well.

Enjoy.

Chef Warren's Bucket List (With a few caveats and explanations.)
Push the edge of the envelope then lick it to induce paper cuts. – *Check*

Learn not to lick the salt off a margarita glass after doing so. - *Check*

Thank former CIA Director, George Tenet, for his leadership at one of the top culinary schools in the world. – *Check*   (Which raised the eyebrows of the other 30 or 40 people present, but brought a smile to Mr. Tenet, who then promised to share his grandmother's recipe for Pastitso with me after the meeting).

Hike and cook along the Appalachian Trail. – *Check*   (When we saw how long that thing was, we decided to just hike a brief section between two mountains in Vermont, the section with a 7-11 right off one of the spurs. Someone forgot the charcoal.)

Learn to spell Appalachian. - *Check*

Become the best banjo player in Florida. – *Check* (Close. Placed second. Not bad for a born and bred New Yorker who wouldn't know grits from a grunt).

Sing background vocals on a Peter, Paul & Mary album. – *Check* (Paul Stookey lived in the neighborhood and he needed some kids to sing background vocals on the album Peter, Paul and Mommy. I was one of the ones who couldn't out-run Mr. Stookey so they dragged me and a bunch of other slow runners to the studio. Yes, that's me in the lower left hand corner of the pic on the back of the album.)

Make my own wine. – *Check*

Make my own vinegar – *Check* (Which is what I got after I failed on my first attempt to make my own wine).

Personally thank Nobel Peace Prize Winner, Desmond Tutu, for his great work in designing all those dresses for little ballerinas. – *Check* (Amid all the accolades he received at that small luncheon, I think mine was the most meaningful to him. At least it seemed so by the roar of his laughter).

Make my own mess. – *Check*

Learn to clean it up. – *Check*

Surround myself with a great family and friends. – *Check.*

Write a novel. – *Check.*

Write a cookbook. – *Check.*

Right a wrong. – *Check.*

Items still on the list:

Visit Ireland.

Eat Jell-O with chopsticks.

Write a sequel to hit movie and memoir, *Julie and Julia* and make it about two women who run a Kosher catering company in Manhattan's diamond district. Call it: *Jewry, Jewelry, Julia and Julie.*

Teach an old dog new tricks.

Learn to speak a foreign language. Like maybe Haiku.

Walk into a frou-frou coffee shop and tell the barista their coffee really does taste like crap.

Live to be 110 just so I can tell folks that daydreaming, single malt Scotch, cookbook-writing, roller coasters, and a strong (but woefully inconsistent) love for God are the keys to a long and happy life.

Now…

What's on your Bucket List that'll likely give you paper cuts?

CHAPTER 35

VARIETY IS THE SPICE OF LIFE

This oft-repeated quote is usually attributed to William Cowper and can be found in his poem: The Task (Book 2, line 285).

While other scholars attribute it to that inimitable Bronx sage, Yogi Berra, who was heard to have said while ordering a pizza at Sal's on West 49th: *"Gimme the works. Extra cheese. Extra sauce. And the more spice. The better. Cuz nothing beats variety except for maybe a little assortment."*

But we'll let the scholars duke that one out. Me? I'm all about variety and spice.

For instance.

I made a Seafood Bisque the other night. Just like I have a gazillion times before. But this time I didn't have any shrimp. So I doubled the oysters and made it anyway. No one complained. In fact, there were a couple of raves.

But *I* knew something was missing because I tasted it with shrimp.

Of course, you've also probably prepared dishes where you were short an ingredient or two. And it's usually the little ingredients. A shot of sherry here. A 1/2 teaspoon of thyme there. One bay leaf instead of two. A dash of hot sauce.

No one usually notices. Except those who've savored the dish in it's completeness.

It's funny how a shot of wine or a pinch or sprinkle of spices and herbs can transform a dish from something that is delicious to one that is extraordinary.

And such is life, eh?

I think about all those brilliant, obnoxious, loving, honest, or grating people who have been a part of my life, even for just a moment, whose influences have transformed what would've been a delicious life into an extraordinary one. Those whose comments, ideas or physical shoves have nudged me into places I may not have ventured into on my own.

Just like that chef who first wondered, "I wonder how a shot of hot sauce would improve this?" And then did it. And then savored it. And then served it to his or her guests.

So the next time I'm preparing a seafood bisque, I'll think about the nuances that other chefs have added based on instinct. And then I'll think about what additions I would make to improve it. Then I'll consider all those who have crossed my path whose words and/or actions have made me what I am today.

And at that point I'm reminded that, perhaps I should let them know.

Perhaps you should, too.

How about this: next week we agree to send a note, drop a line, or send an e-mail to those who have added some spice to our lives. Those whose counsel encouraged us to make monumental decisions. Or those whose word helped us surmount a great obstacle. Or perhaps those whose shoulder invited us to weep when nothing else was available.

I would imagine they would love to hear from the likes of us.

I know I enjoy hearing from those whose lives I've touched (although I rarely knew at the time) in a positive way.

Heck. I know we each have dozens of folk who've nudged and prodded us. Folks who've spiced up and improved our lives.

Now let's spice up theirs by letting them know what a bang up job they did.

Hey, it's just a thought.

Now hand me that cumin and cayenne. I'm ready for a little spice myself tonight.

• QUICK SEAFOOD BISQUE •
(With Variations)

This is a quick bisque that's open to lots of interpretation. If you don't care for oysters, add an equal amount of firm white fish like cod, swordfish or even better, monkfish, then cook until the fish turns opaque. Don't want clams? Add more shrimp. Heck, add whatever seafood you enjoy! I've even made this with a pound and a half of frozen seafood mix I had lying in the freezer.

PREP: 10 minutes   COOK: 15 minutes

INGREDIENTS

1/2 onion, chopped

1 roasted red pepper, chopped (may use jarred)

1 tablespoon unsalted butter

1 (12-ounce) can evaporated milk

1/2 cup half-and-half

1/2 cup dry white wine

1 roasted red pepper, chopped

1 bay leaf

1/4 teaspoon kosher salt

1 dash hot pepper sauce, or more to taste

2 (8-ounce) containers shucked oysters, drained (do not use canned)

2 (6.5 ounce) cans chopped clams with juice

8 ounces medium shrimp, cooked

1 cup chopped portobello mushrooms

1 tablespoon chopped fresh chives to garnish

Hungarian paprika to garnish

DIRECTIONS

1. Melt butter in a small skillet over medium-high heat. Add onions and peppers and sauté until onions are soft and translucent. About 5 - 8 minutes.

2. Meanwhile, heat evaporated milk, half-and-half, white wine, bay leaf, salt, and hot pepper sauce in a large saucepan over medium-low heat, stirring often, until hot but not simmering, about 5 minutes. Stir in the oysters, clams with juice, shrimp and mushrooms. Cover and cook until oysters are just heated through, about 3 minutes. Do not boil.

Remove bay leaf and serve in warm bowls. Sprinkle with chives and paprika to garnish.

CHAPTER 36

GOT A BOOK INSIDE YOU? TRUST ME, YOU MIGHT BE HAPPIER WITH A REALLY GOOD STEAK

When I was at the Book Expo in Manhattan a few years ago, I found myself sitting next to this guy on the subway. You probably know the type: Wall Street...Freshly scrubbed face...Leather satchel...Three piece suit the color of money...

Anyway, we got to talking and he asked me what I did for a living. I told him I was a writer. His eyes lit up and I knew his admiration for me instantly increased.

It always does.

You see, there's something about meeting an actual writer that intrigues people.

Especially women. Beautiful women.

If I had known this 40 years ago, I would've told every girl I met that I was a writer. Even if the only thing I'd written off was my last girlfriend. Why? Because telling a woman that you're a writer ranks right up there with telling her that you work with autistic children.

Or that you train seeing-eye dogs.

Or that you collect food for Somali refugees.

And telling any buxom blonde or sexy brunette that you write seeing-eye dog instructional materials for autistic children in Somalia would no doubt hit the *"I want to have your children"* trifecta.

Unfortunately, I learned this all too late. Now I just impress strangers on subways. Or if I'm lucky, I'll light up the eyes of that three-martini matron at the cocktail party who laments the fact that her recently retired husband just strained his back "leaping to a conclusion."

Ah...if I'd only known then what I know now...

But I digress.

So... I was on the subway chatting with this young-enough-to-be-my-son businessman and told him that I wrote books for a living. After he spent a moment in utter admiration, he sighed and said that, he too, had a book inside him.

Don't we all, I responded.

He said, no, really he really did. Then went on to explain that he'd just eaten a few pages of *War and Peace*. Then he got off at the next stop.

I'm not sure where I'm going with all this. Perhaps it's to say that, if you do have something inside of you that is just dying to get out, then perhaps now is the time to do it. Cookbook. Novel. Short story. Poem. If it's clawing at the door of your soul, perhaps you need to let it loose.

But you must do it right. Otherwise, you might be better off ordering a steak at Peter Luger's.

As in any craft, you'll need to work at it. Sweat over it. Hone it and polish it the best that you can. Offer it up for critique. Rewrite it. Then rewrite it again. Send it to a good editor. Then rewrite it again. But above all, stick with it.

I've met many writers who grew disenchanted because, after a whole two months, their manuscript had received a dozen or so rejection letters from agents. Or their best friend (or even worse, their spouse) laughed and said, "You have something that needs to be said? What happened? Did that gorilla who pounds her fist on the floor to communicate with her trainer die or something?"

Listen, if what you have to say is worth hearing, people will listen. But as in most things, much of it lies in the presentation.

You have a book inside you? Let it sing. But work hard to remove all the sour notes.

You found a recipe that sounds delish? Make it. Then tweak it. Then make it again.

The ladies (or men) will love you for it.

And if you've made a great steak but *really* want to wow your loved one or guests?

 Two words: Compound butter.

It's delish and makes a wonderful presentation. Just place a pat on each steak and let the swooning begin.

Here are some ideas to get you going.

• COMPOUND BUTTER •

I can already hear many of you asking, "Compound butter? I've never seen it in the dairy case at my supermarket. What the heck is it?"

Essentially, compound butter is softened butter, whipped with various herbs, spices and other sweet or savory ingredients. While simple to make, the potential combinations are almost limitless. It's a perfect addition to those of us cooking outside the lines.

And the coolest thing? In addition to a great steak, you can use these on pork, chicken, fish or lamb. Heck, even grilled veggies.

Let's get started!

To make compound butters, start with a stick of unsalted butter. Place it in a bowl and let it sit until it's very soft. To expedite the process, slice it up. When it's soft, stir in the other ingredients until well-mixed. Place the butter mixture onto a sheet of plastic wrap and roll it up to create a nice log. Put it in the fridge to solidify and where it'll keep about 2 weeks. Either that or put it in the freezer to use as needed. It'll last 4 or more months there.

BASIC HERB BUTTER

1 stick unsalted butter, softened

2 tablespoons chopped fresh herbs, such as parsley, thyme, rosemary and oregano. (Or 2 teaspoons dried)

1/2 teaspoon salt

1/2 teaspoon freshly ground pepper

CLASSIC GARLIC BUTTER

1 stick unsalted butter, softened

2 cloves of garlic, minced or pressed

1/4 teaspoon salt

1/4 teaspoon of freshly ground pepper

GARLIC SAGE BUTTER

1 stick unsalted butter, softened

2 tablespoons sage leaves, finely chopped (or 2 teaspoons dried)

2 cloves garlic, minced or pressed

1/4 teaspoon salt

GORGONZOLA OR BLEU CHEESE BUTTER

1 stick unsalted butter, softened

1/2 cup (4-ounces) crumbled Gorgonzola or blue cheese

2 tablespoons chopped fresh parsley (or 2 teaspoons dried)

1/2 teaspoon salt

GORGONZOLA SAGE BUTTER

1 stick unsalted butter, softened

1/2 cup (4-ounces) crumbled Gorgonzola or blue cheese

1 tablespoon minced fresh sage (or 1 teaspoon dried)

1/2 teaspoon salt

BLACK PEPPER AND MUSHROOM BUTTER

1 stick unsalted butter, softened

10 dried shitake mushrooms, soaked in water until soft, then drained and chopped

1 tablespoon coarsely ground black pepper

SUN DRIED TOMATO BUTTER

1 stick unsalted butter, softened

2 tablespoons chopped fresh parsley (or 2 teaspoons dried)

1 clove garlic, minced or pressed

2 tablespoons sun-dried tomatoes chopped

1/2 teaspoon salt

SMOKED PAPRIKA & ROSEMARY BUTTER

1 stick unsalted butter

1 tablespoon minced fresh rosemary, crumbled (or 1 teaspoon dried)

1 teaspoon smoked paprika

1/2 teaspoon salt

SPICY MUSTARD BUTTER

1 stick unsalted butter

2 teaspoons Dijon mustard

1/4 teaspoon cayenne pepper

2 tablespoons chopped fresh parsley (or 2 teaspoons dried)

JALAPENO LIME BUTTER

1 stick unsalted butter, softened

1 jalapeno pepper, seeded, and finely minced (use half a jalapeno for less heat)

2 teaspoons finely chopped fresh cilantro

1 tablespoon fresh lime juice

1/2 teaspoon salt

1/4 teaspoon freshly ground black pepper

CHIPOTLE LIME BUTTER

1 stick unsalted butter

1 teaspoon chipotle powder (or ancho chili powder)

1/2 teaspoon lime zest

BACON AND BOURBON BUTTER

1 stick unsalted butter, softened

2 slices smoked bacon, cooked and chopped

1 tablespoon bourbon

1 tablespoon real maple syrup

CHAPTER 37

FOOD WISDOM FROM THE ANCIENTS. AND THEN SOME

As I flit about the Foodie Cybersphere, I can't help but love all the pithy food quotes that people are wont to post. Including me.

They bring a smile to my face and a warm feeling to my tummy. I love the classics like:

"Nothing would be more tiresome than eating and drinking if God had not made them a pleasure as well as a necessity." ~ Voltaire

or

"Noncooks think it's silly to invest two hours' work in two minutes' enjoyment; but if cooking is evanescent, so is the ballet." ~ Julia Child

or

"My favorite vegetable is steak" ~ Fran Lebowitz

or

"The trouble with eating Italian food is that five or six days later you're hungry again." ~ George Miller

But as an avid food writer, sometimes I yearn for something deeper. Something beyond the norm.

I want to hear the voices of the ancients who have trod the path before me. To glean from their wisdom. Learn from their experience.

But how?!

I knew it wouldn't be easy. I had to gather together those steeped in the ancient disciplines. Like:

Linguistics. My good friend Charisse loves linguini. No joke. And she can kick butt on any one of a dozen linguini dishes. (Her puttanesca? To die for!) So I guess I have a linguist in my corner.

Archaeology. I went to college with a guy who now plays a pirate on Captain Nemo's Pirate Ship down at the pier. Sure, he's getting a bit on in years, but he can growl "Argh" with the best of them. Man, that dude can put the ''Argh'' in Archaeologist. So I guess I have that covered.

A great Epicurean. I don't go to the movies much any more (ever since they put that padlock on the alley door) so I rarely ever get to see the epics. Films like the

X-Men franchise, Iron Man, Captain America, or the final Harry Potter. But my friend Ron sees all the epics. He even buys tickets to romantic comedies. Heck, he even sees the jive-ass slapstick crap that wouldn't even rate as sitcoms. But he goes nuts over the blockbuster epics. So I guess I have an Epicurean on board.

Next, I needed a wine expert. That would be an oenologist. But since I can't spell it or even say it on a consistent basis (especially after a glass or two of wine) I knew I might have trouble locating an actual wine expert and would have to settle for someone who was just a really good whiner. That would be my friend, Bart, whose wife ran off with a juggler from the circus and whose son just converted to Scientology so he can jump up and down on a late night TV show couch just like Tom Cruise. And last Saturday, his daughter booked a room at the Plaza for a mad night of passion with a recently paroled purse snatcher she met on Facebook. Oh, and Bart just bought a Yugo with low miles on Craig's List. So yes, I do believe Bart can whine with the best of them. He's in.

So the five of us committed ourselves to bringing you the crème de la crème of the ancients.

Oh, and what we found when we combined efforts! I hope the wisdom of these elders inspires you like it did us.

Wisdom from the Ancients

"Berries picked at dawn will nourish those who dine at noon. Berries picked at eve won't. Sorry." ~ Etched on the Sixth Obelisk at Stonehenge.

"I despaired that I had no eating utensils. Then I met a man that had no arms. So I said, "Since you probably won't be using that fork…" From the Fourth Writings of the Upurarse, 174 BC

"I climbed the Big Rock Candy Mountain seeking knowledge. I met a wise lollipop on a lonesome road and asked, "What must I do to find enlightenment?" The lollipop smiled, and with a twinkling eye replied, "Suck me." ~ From the writings of Diu Mi, Fourth Dynasty, 27 BC

"An olive and a bit of cheese on the tongue of a poor man is better than a cup of Venti Starbucks left on the roof of a Porsche as the owner darted out of the lot late for yet another stupid meeting. Verily, amen." ~ Corporitus Interruptus, 99 AD

"On a chill as winter's evening there's nothing quite like a hot bowl of soup. No wait. A steaming bowl of water with some bits of vegetables in it is a lot like a bowl of soup. Never mind." ~ St. Gastronome the Obvious, 515 AD

"Preparing a meal for your loved ones reflects the mighty miracle of Jesus feeding the 5000. Except there are probably 4,995 fewer of you. More or less." ~ Pope Flavorius, 949 AD

"A fine, fatted, fowl fit for the fourth Friday of February is much easier said once than three times fast." ~ St. Stu the st...st...st...Stutterer ~ 1349 AD

"Canadian bacon is neither Canadian, nor bacon. But it sure makes a one hell of an Egg McMuffin." ~ Sir Ronald McDonald, 1982 AD

"If it weren't for Evander Holyfield's tasty ears, I would've become a vegetarian much sooner." ~ Mike Tyson, 1997

"God created whiskey to keep the Irish from taking over the world. And God created haggis to keep the Scots from going into the restaurant business." ~ St. Warren the Wiseguy, 2019 AD

Now...what ancient wisdom have you gleaned lately?

CHAPTER 38
DON'T TRY THIS AT HOME AND OTHER STUPID ADVICE

In the last chapter, I offered some time-tested and truly useful culinary advice from the ancients.

Pearls of wisdom gleaned from mist-enshrouded fields of Stonehenge, mysterious ancient Chinese dynasties, dank medieval monasteries, and the steamy, bustling kitchens of five-star restaurants...not to mention the twisted mind of the bonehead that puts pen to paper and writes cookbooks in the discomfort of his overheated office. (That would be me.)

And yet, a lot of dubious advice still finds its way onto the Internet. Some I was able to tweak and make work (yes, one can cook eggs in a microwave oven, but you must take them out of the shells first.)

But much of it I tried and found wanting (you can't cook Minute Rice® in the microwave and expect it to be done in 10 seconds.)

And some of the advice was so inanely stupid (you can't cram yourself into a microwave oven and expect to go into the future) that I had to file it away in that part of my brain that the French gourmands gleefully refer to as *"Le Grande Toilette."*

Perhaps you've seen some of these and filed them away as well. But silly advice isn't limited to cooking. There's lots of advice floating around that just relates to life in general. The trouble is, some of this advice seem to make sense on the surface, but when given some thought, may not really be helpful. Here are but a few:

"If you can dream it, you can do it." ~ **Walt Disney**

Okay. Last week I dreamt that I met Scarlett Johansson at one of my cooking demos and she invited me up to her suite to, um, butter her crepes. Needless to say, I haven't done that yet. (And if my dear wife has anything to say about it, I probably never will.) Boy, talk about Mickey Mouse dreams, Walt.

"Do what you love and the money will follow." ~ **Numerous motivational speakers.**

Do what you love and the money will follow? My friend Summer loves to post every ten seconds of her life on Facebook. (Did you read the recent updates about her struggle over whether to buy the Sperry Top-Sider Silverside shoes or the Sperry Top-Sider Fairwinds? No? Then count yourself as one of the blessed.) Anyway, she hasn't made enough posting on Facebook to quit her job at Wendy's even though she's been at it for a couple of years now. So if the money's following her, it must've stopped to ask directions along the way. And don't get me started on my friend, Bo, who loves to play Black Ops on Xbox for days on end. The money's still looking for him, too.

"Don't try this at home." ~ **Super Dave Osborne and various other daredevils**

Listen. As far as I'm concerned, if you can't try it in the privacy of your own home, where else are you gonna try it? The ballet? The corner market? The boss' house? Geez, the last time I actually heard this lamebrain exhortation was from a street performer who was about to eat a flaming sword. I mean, if you're going to try something like that, are you going to do so in a day care center? A nursing home? Your child custody trial? No way. You better darn well try that nonsense at home.

And here's one of my favorites:

"Drink red wine with meat and white wine with fish or fowl." ~ **Numerous gastronomes**

Oh puh-lease. Who invented this stuff? Probably the same group of folk who came up with some of the other bewildering rules like: "Don't mix your metaphors" as if saying that one shouldn't put all their chickens in one basket before they hatch a plan to look before they leap for one giant step for mankind, or whatever.

Listen. Food is all about taste and what pleases you and your friends.

Do you or any of your guests enjoy Pinot Grigio with beef? Merlot with snapper? Go for it!

Do you have a hankering for pasta, potatoes and rice all at the same time? Then screw the starch witches and whip up a frittata with all three ingredients!

Sauté onions and garlic together until the onions become soft and translucent like so many cookbooks say? Don't! If you sauté them both together, the garlic will be done way before the onions. Instead, sauté your onions for 5 to 8 minutes first, then add your garlic and sauté a minute or two more. Your taste buds will love you for it!

I'm getting carried away here. Sorry.

But when it comes to great advice that really does make sense, you gotta love this piece of eternal wisdom:

"Be who you are and say what you feel because those who mind don't matter and those who matter don't mind." ~ **Dr. Seuss**

Now, how 'bout pouring me a glass of that Cab to go along with my grilled fish…

• GRILLED TUNA WITH GARLIC-LEMON SAUCE •

(Tonna alla Siciliana)

I like this healthy dish because it's not only lightning quick to make, but is open to variations. You can make this with tuna, swordfish or salmon, and you can cook it on the grill or in a skillet.

PREP: 10 minutes   MARINATE: 5 minutes
COOK: 6 minutes

INGREDIENTS
   2 (6 - 8 ounce) tuna steaks (or swordfish or salmon)
   1 lemon, finely zested and juiced
   2 tablespoon chopped fresh Italian leaf parsley
   3 cloves garlic, minced or pressed
   1 teaspoon oregano
   1/2 teaspoon dried chili pepper, or less to taste
   7 tablespoons extra virgin olive oil, divided
   2 tablespoons water (or white wine)
   Kosher salt and freshly ground pepper to taste

DIRECTIONS
   1.   Prepare a grill for medium high heat.

   2.   In a small bowl, combine the lemon zest lemon juice, 1 tablespoon parsley, garlic, chili pepper, 6 tablespoons olive oil, and water. Stir briskly to mix.

   3.   Brush the steaks on both sides with half the sauce and let marinate for 5 minutes.

   4.   Lightly oil grill or preheat a 10-inch skillet over medium high heat, add the olive and swirl to coat. Place the steaks on the grill or in the skillet and cook until the white line that develops where the steak meets the heat comes up about 1/4 of the way up the side of the steak. Turn and cook until the white line comes up about 1/4 the way up the other side (for swordfish or salmon, cook until just cooked through but still moist in the center, about 3 – 4 minutes per side.

   5.   Spoon remaining sauce over steaks and season with salt and pepper to taste. Garnish with the remaining parsley.

COOKING OUTSIDE THE LINES VARIATIONS

We already talked about using other thick and meaty fish, like swordfish or salmon. But you can use this on chicken breasts and thighs, pork chops, or pork tenderloin sliced into medallions.

Here are some other options:

- Substitute the basil, tarragon, marjoram, or any other favorite herb for the oregano.

- Add 1/2 teaspoon smoked paprika for an earthier, smokier flavor.

- Add a teaspoon or two of balsamic vinegar for depth.

- Add a tablespoon of fresh lime, lemon, or even orange juice for brightness.

CHAPTER 39

YOU COULD BATHE A SMALL CHILD IN THAT MARGARITA. BUT THE SINK WOULD BE CHEAPER

My wife and I visited Miami Beach a number of years ago. If it wasn't due to the fact that Kassav was scheduled to play at the Jackie Gleason Theater, we wouldn't have even considered submitting ourselves to the stifling mid-July heat and humidity that turns the South Florida air into molten Jell-O.

Frying eggs on the sidewalk? Ha, mere child's play. We saw two guys grilling brats in mid-air as we drove by Flamingo Park.

Anyway, we checked into our hotel at four pm then wandered down to Ocean Drive to scope things out. For those of you who have never visited South Beach, Ocean Drive is flanked by beachfront Lummus Park to the east and three-story art deco hotels clad in the pastel colors that made Miami Vice famous to the west. The hotels also house cafés that spill out of their lobbies and onto the sidewalk where umbrellas the size of flying saucers shield diners from the blazing sun. Since the sidewalks are clustered with tables, it only leaves narrow pathways for pedestrians to amble through in single file. Two can walk abreast if they are anorexic. Severely overweight tourists are forced to use the street.

Most of these cafés also feature gorgeous, but aggressive young women with mysterious accents accosting passersby with discount cards for lunch, dinner and 2-for-1 drinks. We had only walked two or three blocks, eluding the grasp of these young waifs, when the heat and humidity began to take its toll. We were parched. The constant sight of couples nursing drinks under the shade of billowing umbrellas didn't help. And, oh, what drinks! I know it was only an illusion created by the clever shape of the glasses (wide as a hubcap but shallow as a thimble) but they still looked like you could bathe a small child in one. As sweat pooled around our feet and soaked into our flip-flops, we decided it was time to dive into one of these enormous margaritas.

We were in luck. The next café had a few empty tables. The girl manning the sidewalk released her grip on a fleeing family of five and greeted us in an English dialect that could only have been acquired from a childhood spent raking dirt on a farm in a former Soviet Socialist Republic that surely ended in "-stan."

"Two for table? Dinner?" she asked with a smile as bright as the sun.

"No. Just drinks," I replied, my lips puckering at the thought of cool lime-infused tequila washing over my taste buds. "The 2-for-1 special."

"This way," she said as she led us through a sea of couples enjoying their frozen concoctions. But just before we sat down, I did something I've never done in a bar or café.

I asked her how much the drinks were.

I don't know what drove me to it. I've been in lots of bars from Orlando to New York to Chicago to L.A. I've had $15 dollar martinis off Central Park and $2 bottles of PBR in Portland. I figured South Beach would be at the upper end. Maybe $10 for what must surely be a mostly-fruit-juice margarita. But still, I asked.

"So. How much are the drinks?"

"How much?" our petite hostess echoed, scrunching up her nose as if that sort of question had not been covered in training.

"Yes. For a Margarita."

"29 dollars."

I gasped.

"Not counting taxes and tip," she added.

I crunched the numbers in my head. $29 for the drink. 7% sales tax. 2% food and beverage tax. 1% homeless and domestic violence tax on food and beverage. Then the 20% tip that is automatically and inexplicably added to all tabs in South Beach regardless of the service. Some cafés even add a surcharge that goes to their favorite charity. This establishment did.

It came out to 40 bucks.

But we were hot. We were in the shade. We were on vacation. And it *was* 2-for-1. We certainly could spare $20 a piece for a large margarita, couldn't we?

I pulled out a chair and found myself saying, "Okay. We'll take the 2-for-1 one special. I'll have one. My wife will have the other."

"Sorry. No sharing. One drink special per customer. You each have to buy one."

"Huh?"

She waved her hand toward the other restaurants that dotted the boulevard. "Everywhere the same. This is South Beach."

The calculator in my mind whirred and buzzed. 80 bucks for two orders of margaritas? I looked around at the other tourists enjoying their drinks and wondered if they knew how much their final tab would be. I shuddered as I heard a couple to my left order a second round.

Cha-ching. $160 worth of drinks for those two.

To my right, a Fabio-look-alike leapt to his feet and tossed his chair aside while screaming something that vaguely sounded like Portuguese. The woman with him looked mortified.

I assumed he had just received his tab. Oh, my. Looks like they'd ordered appetizers, too. Ouch.

I turned back to our hostess. "No thanks," I said.

We wound our way back out to the sidewalk and continued our journey south until we spotted a lonely café off the beaten path. A waiter clearing tables out front invited us in for the 'mojito drink special'.

I smirked. "How much?"

"5 bucks."

I smiled, grabbed my wife's hand and wandered into the cool and shade.

Sometimes it pays to ask.

Here are some recipes for a few South Beach classics. And they won't set you back $40.

• CLASSIC MARGARITA FOR ONE •

I know you can buy bottles of margarita mix. In fact, margaritas made from mix are what most of us are accustomed to. It's what restaurants use. And although it'll do in a pinch, or if you're throwing a large party, there's nothing quite like a margarita made from scratch. Here's one such recipe. It'll cost a tad more to make it from scratch than from a mix. But be careful, once you taste it, you may never go back to a mix again.

INGREDIENTS
   Kosher salt for rimming the glasses
   1-1/2 ounces good tequila
   1 ounce fresh lime juice
   1/2 ounce Cointreau (or Triple Sec for a sweeter margarita)
   Fresh lime slices for garnish

DIRECTIONS
   1. Place the salt in a shallow dish or saucer. Moisten the rim of the glass with a slice of lime then dip into the salt.

   2. Fill the glass with ice (crushed is optional). Add tequila, lime juice and Cointreau. Stir until chilled. Garnish with a slice of lime and serve immediately.

• CLASSIC MOJITO FOR ONE •

INGREDIENTS

2 ounces white rum

2 tablespoons fresh lime juice (save the peel)

2 teaspoons superfine sugar

15 mint leaves, divided

1 cup cracked ice

Splash of club soda or seltzer

DIRECTIONS

1. In Tom Collins glass, stir the lime juice with the sugar until it dissolves. Add 12 mint leaves, mashing them against the side of the glass.

3. Fill glass 2/3 full with cracked ice and pour in the rum. Stir gently for 15 seconds.

4. Add the squeezed-out lime shell and top off with club soda or seltzer. Garnish with 3 fresh mint leaves.

• CLASSIC PINA COLADA FOR ONE •

INGREDIENTS

1-1/2 ounces dark rum

2 ounces cream of coconut

2 ounces pineapple juice

Maraschino cherry, for garnish

DIRECTIONS

1. Add 1 cup ice to blender; add remaining ingredients (except garnish).

2. Blend until smooth.

3. Pour into a highball glass and garnish with a cherry.

• CLASSIC PLANTER'S PUNCH FOR ONE •

INGREDIENTS
  1-½ ounces dark rum
  2 teaspoons grenadine
  2 ounces (1/4-cup) pineapple juice
  Splash of club soda or seltzer

DIRECTIONS
  1. Mix ingredients together, and pour over ice. Add a splash of club soda, if
      you want.

• CUBA LIBRE FOR ONE •

INGREDIENTS
  1/2 lime
  2 ounces rum
  4 ounces Coke

DIRECTIONS
  1. Squeeze the lime into a tall glass (Tom Collins or highball glass). Drop the lime
      into the glass and muddle it to release the citrus oil. Remove the lime and
      add ice, rum and coke. Stir well and enjoy!

CHAPTER 40

SOUTH BEACH, PART TWO: KILLER DEALS, CHEAP EATS, AND FILCHING THE COMPLIMENTARY LEMONADE

I discovered Miami's Townhouse Hotel on the Internet. On TripAdvisor to be exact.

Okay. I confess. I'm one of those nerds who scour the World Wide Web looking for killer travel deals that could only be explained as being posted by disgruntled employees intent on driving their employers to bankruptcy. I'm talking about incredible deals. Killer deals. Obscene deals. Like buy "two nights get four free" kind of deals.

Of course, several friends (…okay…*many* friends) think this kind of cyber sleuthing is a complete waste of time. They feel I should be spending my limited free hours on something more productive. Things they like to do. Like playing video games.

But no. This is my hobby, thank you very much. And unlike other people's addictive and life-sapping suburban hobbies like fantasy football, internet porn, and growing vegetables from scratch in that weed-infested plot of land most folks call "the backyard", my hobby actually pays real dividends. Whenever one of my friends rags on me for spending so many hours hunkered down in front of the blue light of my laptop, I ask them when was the last time they scored a $450-per-night boutique hotel room with a full kitchen in Midtown Manhattan for $90 a night? Oops. Did I hear "never"? All right then.

So a couple of weeks before our scheduled trip to Miami, I snuggled up to the computer with a glass of wine, began my search, and made reservations.

We checked into our hotel just north of South Beach (which is also known as SoBe) in an area called Miami Modern (also known as MiMo). However, this area is not to be confused with the mainland Miami Modern section on Biscayne Boulevard (also known as MiMo BiBo). No. We were staying in that part of Miami Beach that showcases the grand architecture of Morris Lapidus and Norman Giller. Think Fontainebleau, Eden Roc, the Delano, or the Carillon.

We opted to stay at the less prestigious, but infinitely more affordable, Townhouse, which is located in a subsection of MiMo called Low Cost Miami Modern (also known as LoCo MiMo). While not situated directly on the beach (it's a mere half block away), the Townhouse makes up for it with a stunning rooftop venue arrayed with enormous red and white striped umbrellas and lounges the size of inflatable life rafts. At least that's what the pictures on the Website depicted. The rooftop lounge would have made for several delightfully romantic evenings had it not been closed and under renovation. Oh well, at least there was a sushi bar in the basement.

But since I'm not an ardent fan of sushi (preferring jelly rolls to California rolls), I brushed aside that option to explore some of the other venues/activities I'd found on the Internet. Here are a few nice options:

The Townhouse, of course. Which, in spite of the fact that the rooftop lounge was closed, had a pretty funky vibe and a great continental breakfast. Not to mention the retro beach bikes they have for rent in case the brand new bikes you brought with you get stolen in broad daylight on a busy street even though they were secured with an elephant chain and industrial-grade padlocks. (Note to self: next time attach a miniature explosive to the bike lock.)

Christine Michaels' Art Deco Walking Tour. Christine's genuine enthusiasm, irresistible charm, and extensive knowledge raise her Art Deco Tour above just about any other tour I have taken. Plus, she's prettier than the guy leading the 'other' Deco walking tour.

Café Charlotte. This little hole-in-the-wall storefront restaurant serves up remarkably delicious Venezuelan/Argentine food at a terrific price. No pretense or attitude. It's easy to miss, so keep an eye out.

The renovated Fontainebleau. We wandered through this stunning ode to mid-century excess like we owned the joint, helping ourselves to the complimentary fresh-squeezed lemonade.

Puerto Sagua Restaurant. This is a local joint in every sense of the word. It's always packed but they seem to find a place for everybody since turnover is quick. Great Cuban comfort food at a remarkably reasonable price.

Spiga Ristorante Italiano. From the quiet ambiance to the delicious entrées to the attentive wait staff, Spiga sets itself apart from most of the other SoBe restaurants in its price range. It was our anniversary.

The Boardwalk. Riding bikes with the ocean breeze at our backs and the sun on our shoulders.

Front Porch Café and Tropical Beach Café. Delicious and filling homemade breakfasts at both of these spots.

Now, when you think about the $80 we could've shelled out for a round of margaritas (see previous chapter), I think we came out ahead, don't you?

And while we're talking about eating well, but on the cheap, here's my take on a dish for which Café Charlotte is noted. Enjoy with your homemade Sangria (page 69).

• PABELLON CRIOLLO A CABALLO •

Pabellon Criollo is Venezuela's national, and certainly most popular, dish. It's loosely translated as "Creole Flag" because, when it's served, with the shredded beef on the left of the plate, the steamed rice in the middle, and the black beans to the right, it resembles the Venezuelan flag. "A caballo" simply means "on horseback" and refers to the optional fried egg topping. This looks like it takes some time to make, but remember, most of the cooking time is spent simmering the beef. And because it takes a while to make, we're making more than is needed to feed two people – you're gonna love the leftovers (makes great sandwiches!) Just divide into zip lock bags and freeze.

PREP: 15 minutes   COOK: 1-1/2 hours

INGREDIENTS
   2 pounds flank steak

   1/4 cup olive oil

   2 cups chopped onion

   1 bay leaf

   5 cups beef broth

   1 red bell pepper, chopped

   3 cloves garlic, minced or crushed

   ½ teaspoon ground cumin

   1 teaspoon oregano

   1 (15-ounce) can chopped tomatoes

   Kosher salt and freshly ground pepper to taste

   1 egg for each serving

DIRECTIONS
1.   Heat 2 tablespoons olive oil in a skillet over medium-high heat. Pat dry steak and sear on both sides until brown, about 4 – 5 minutes per side.

2.   Remove from skillet and place in a large pot or Dutch oven with 1 cup chopped onion, bay leaf and enough beef broth to cover (about 5 cups). Bring to a boil over high heat, then reduce heat to low. Cover and simmer for 1 to 1-1/2 hours until meat is very tender.

3.   Remove the meat and set aside to cool. Strain the broth and reserve. When the meat is cooled a bit, shred with your fingers or a fork.

4. Reheat the skillet over medium-heat and add remaining olive oil. Add the remaining chopped onion and the red pepper. Sauté until the onions are soft and translucent, about 8 – 10 minutes. Stir in the garlic, cumin and oregano and sauté 1 – 2 additional minutes.

5. Stir in the shredded meat, chopped tomatoes and kosher salt and freshly ground pepper to taste. Add enough reserved broth to moisten the mixture (you may freeze remaining broth for other uses). Simmer for 15 – 20 minutes, adding broth as necessary to keep the mixture moist.

6. Meanwhile, fry an egg for each serving.

7. Top each portion of flank steak with a fried egg.

• FRIED PLANTAINS •

PREP: Less than 5 minutes   COOK: 10 minutess

Sure, they may look like bananas, but they are very different. Unlike bananas, you want to buy plantains that are yellow-green to cook with. If you want a sweeter plantain, let them ripen until they are almost black. I found the best way to peel them is to cut off each end then carefully slice through the skin length-wise without cutting into the flesh.

INGREDIENTS
   1 - 2 plantains, peeled
   1 cup +/- vegetable or peanut oil (enough to fill skillet 1-inch)
   Kosher salt and freshly ground pepper to taste

DIRECTIONS
   1. Slice the plantains cross-wise at a diagonal, about 1/2-inch thick

   2. Heat 1-inch oil in a 10-inch skillet over medium- high heat.

   3. Place plantains in the skillet and sauté until the bottom is golden brown, about 5 - 8 minutes. Turn and sauté for another 5 minutes until golden brown. Season with salt and pepper.

• STEAMED WHITE RICE •

Will make enough for some leftovers.

PREP: 5 minutes   COOK: 20 minutes

INGREDIENTS
   1-1/2 cups long grain rice
   2-1/4 cups water
   2 tablespoons unsalted butter, divided
   Kosher salt and freshly ground pepper to taste

DIRECTIONS
   1.   Melt 1 tablespoon butter in a medium saucepan over medium heat. Add the
        rice and stir until nicely coated. Increase the heat to medium-high and add
        the water. Bring to a boil and cover.

   2.   Reduce heat to medium-low and simmer until rice is tender and the water
        has evaporated, about 18 minutes. Remove the saucepan from the heat and
        let sit for 5 minutes. Add remaining butter and stir to fluff. Season with salt
        and pepper to taste.

• EASIEST BLACK BEANS •

I have several wonderful recipes for black beans. Many of them require quite a few ingredients and, if made with dried beans, could take a couple of hours or more to prepare. Here, we're going to make a very simple, yet tasty, black bean side dish that pairs well with our savory entrée. Note: feel free to add one chopped red or green pepper when you sauté the onions. I didn't include them here because we're using pepper in the entrée.

PREP: 10 minutes   COOK: 35 minutes

INGREDIENTS
- 2 cans black beans, undrained
- 1 tablespoon olive or canola oil
- 1 medium onion, chopped (about 1 cup)
- 4 cloves garlic, minced or pressed
- 1 teaspoon cumin
- 1/2 teaspoon oregano
- 1/2 teaspoon salt
- 1/4 teaspoon freshly ground pepper (or more to taste)

DIRECTIONS
1. Heat the olive oil in a medium saucepan over medium heat. Add the onions and sauté until soft, about 8 minutes. Add the garlic and sauté until fragrant and slightly golden, about 1 – 2 additional minutes.

2. Stir in the beans and liquid, cumin, oregano, salt and pepper. Simmer, stirring occasionally, for 20 – 25 minutes so flavors meld.

CHAPTER 41

FIVE KITCHEN DEVICES THAT SHOULD ONLY BE USED FOR ONE THING

If you've followed my writing for any length of time, you know I'm not overly fond of kitchen gadgets that are only good for one specific task. I'm thinking about items like the "*Duraworks String Bean String Extractor*", or "*Chef Jimmy's Carolina Pork Rind Warmer*", or "*CalCo Dry Spaghetti Breaker.*"

I like items that have multiple purposes even if I have to come up with the ideas myself. I mean, who among us hasn't pounded chicken breasts flat with a big can of spaghetti sauce, a large cookbook, or Uncle Andy's wooden leg (but only when he's napping)?

Face it; I just don't like kitchen clutter, so I make it a point to buy items that multi-task. However, there are some kitchen devices that are pretty much good for only one thing and one thing only. To use them for unintended purposes could result in injury, death or a ton of embarrassment at your next big shindig.

Using the icemaker to create frozen daiquiris. Most people dislike the fact that frozen daiquiris become diluted as the ice melts. Some of us have tried to circumvent the problem by hooking up vats of rum-infused daiquiri mix to our icemaker lines. Only one problem: You need lots of water pressure to make it work. Petitioning the water company to add a second "booze line" is a waste of time. Just ask the citizens of Key West. (However, I understand some Caribbean countries, like Barbados, have a two-spigot system. One for white rum, and the other for dark rum.) The only other alternative is to mount a small cistern on your roof and fill it full of booze. The force of gravity should be enough to fill your ice machine. The downside is that you have to climb up onto the roof to refill it when it runs dry. Not a good idea if your party is just hitting its stride and you've already downed a couple of daiquiris yourself.

Oh, and as an aside, stapling two wires to the cistern and running them down to the back of your flat screen TV will not provide you with free satellite TV.

Tried it. Didn't work.

Using the microwave oven to take out the chill in a room. There's a reason they put that screen with little holes in it on the microwave door. And there's a reason they installed a switch that won't allow the oven to operate unless the door is closed. You see, a microwave oven creates heat by "exciting" the molecules in water and fat. Remember, human beings are 98% water (and many of us are also

98% fat), so bypassing the switch the microwave door will warm things up a bit... but not the way you or any of your guests standing near the open door expect.

You feeling chilly? Grab a butter knife and stick it the nearest electrical outlet. It's faster and cheaper.

Opening the fridge and freezer door to cool off a hot kitchen. This one really needs no comment. We've all tried it. We all learned it didn't work.

Using the electric knife sharpener on other utensils. Knife sharpeners are great for knives. (Everyone knows a sharp knife is a safe knife.) But it's not good for forks and spoons. Think about it; when was the last time anyone ever complained that your forks weren't sharp enough? Of course, if one of my dinner guests did just that, I'd ask them to repeat it. Then I'd stab them in the hand while asking, "Sharp enough for you, Bob?"

And, although, the idea that a razor sharp ice cream scoop would get the ice cream out of the box quicker, the risk of injury from a utensil that's not normally regarded as "sharp" runs very high. Especially if you have kids. Or anyone in your house that suffers from "the shakes."

Using the garbage disposal as a blender. You'd think that a two-horsepower device that can grind pork chop bones into tiny pieces would be an ideal blender, especially for margaritas and daiquiris. Forget it. Everything you put in it just winds up going down the drain.

Of course, one could temporarily disconnect the plumbing so that the disposal drains into a pitcher. But it still may not be a good idea. Particularly, if you recently used it to grind up a bunch of pork chop bones. No one likes having to use a toothpick after drinking a margarita. Trust me on that.

Using the exhaust fan above the stove to chop veggies. Removing the filter screen and using the fan as a vegetable chopper is a better idea in concept than it is in real life. (It especially sounded like a great idea after I downed a couple of garbage disposal margaritas.) I mean what could be easier? Just put a big bowl on the stove under the fan, flip that baby on, and hurl some carrots, onions or celery up into it. Right? Wrong. You see, while some of the pieces will fall back into the bowl, most of the pieces will go right out the vent. Which would be a bummer if your vent empties out anywhere near the neighbor's Jacuzzi.

So how 'bout you? Have you ever tried using a kitchen device for unintended purposes? What were the results? I'm sure other readers (and ambulance-chasing attorneys) are anxious to hear about your experiences.

CHAPTER 42

STATE FAIR FOOD (OR: WHY SHOULD I BOTHER WEARING SEAT BELTS ON A RAIN-SLICK MOUNTAIN ROAD)

As we ease out of August and enter the fall season, many of us will be drawn to the cool outdoors. Some of us will long to go hiking in the woods, some of us will fill the stands of our favorite football teams, and some of us will make plans to revel in that great American institution: the state fair.

At one time, state fairs focused on livestock, produce, and the joyful simplicities of rural life. Sure there was a midway where gaudy portable rides offered a few cheap thrills for the kids, but the highlight was usually the competitions, where friends and neighbors vied for the fattest pig or the best apple pie.

I'm know state fairs still include the tradition of competitions, but these events aren't as well attended as they were in days past. Even the Midway has undergone a metamorphosis: classic rides like the merry-go-round and Tilt-a-Whirl have been replaced by contraptions constructed by itinerant workers whose skills would make them more usefully employed as dirt sifters, furniture testers, or U.S. Senators. I'm thinking mind-numbing rides like The Mutant, The Bone Crusher, or The Kiddie Coaster with Six Missing Critical Bolts.

But by far, one of the most popular draws is the fun food. Whereas fair-going families of yore relished normally forbidden treats like crisp and juicy corn dogs, pillows of cotton candy, or caramel apples the size of softballs, today's modern fair-goer is introduced to food that would've baffled even the most adventurous diner of days gone by. I'm sure you've seen, and perhaps tasted, some of these artery-clogging creations. I offer here just a few, along with improved variations that I feel would be "more tempting to the masses while fattening their asses." Or what I've formally dubbed, "Warren's Mass of Ass State Fair Snacks."

I mean why careen down a rain-slick mountain road without seat belts when you can cut the brake lines before doing so, thus ensuring a more entertaining and satisfying trip? So why settle for deep fried snickers bars when you can opt for deep fried Oreo stuffed Twinkies.

State Fair Standard Midway Food:

Deep Fried Snickers Bars. These candy bars (one of my favorites when I was a kid) already boast 29 grams of sugar and top out at 266 calories, so why would someone deep fry them and coat them with sugar? Because they can. Now this little treat boasts 700 calories. That's more than three slices of pepperoni cheese pizza.

Chef Warren's Mass of Ass Improvement:

Glazed Deep Fried Oreo-Stuffed Twinkies with Sprinkles. Deep Fried Oreos and their cousin, Deep Fried Twinkies, have become state fair staples, so why not combine them and coat them with a sugary glaze and a fistful of colorful sprinkles? Boo-yeah. Now we're batting 1,000 (calories, that is.)

State Fair Standard:

Krispy Kreme Burgers. Created in the deep South and popularized by Paula Deen, this concoction features a quarter pound beef patty topped with cheese and bacon then sandwiched between two buttered halves of a Krispy Kreme Donut. Some calorie counters peg it at 500 calorie, and some at over 1,000. Of course, the real question is, how do you dunk that sucker?

Chef Warren's Mass of Ass Improvement:

Double Fried Krispy Kreme Meatball Subs. Face it, many fair goers still feel hungry after eating the Krispy Kreme Burger. For those whose cravings exceed the calorie count of one of these standards, we offer the ultimate state fair sub where ground beef and a beef-like product are molded into globes the size of tennis balls, wrapped in bacon, then deep fried. These are topped with tomato sauce, fried onions, fried green peppers, and 11 different cheeses (fried lettuce is available on request) and sandwiched between four halved Krispy Kreme Donuts before the whole sandwich is deep fried again. The best part? No need to dunk. Problem solved.

State Fair Standard:

Deep Fried Butter on a Stick. This is one of the latest fads on the state fair circuit. Balls of butter are coated in batter and deep-fried until the outside is crisp. Fans liken it to a croissant with a more buttery taste. Croissant? Um, right. I think I hear the French surrendering. Again.

Chef Warren's Mass of Ass Improvement:

Lard on a Candy Cane. Why go through the hassle of preparing a batch of coating and firing up the deep fat fryer? Cut down on time without cutting calories with a big hunk of lard impaled on a candy cane.

Y'know, now that I think about it, it appears that people in general will eat anything if it's deep fried, so why don't vendors skip the food wholesaler altogether and deep fry items that they won't even cost them anything? Items that are readily available for free in any community? Talk about pure profit! I've already invented several. Please don't drool on your cookbook.

Warren's New Ultra-Profitable Mass of Ass State Fair Snacks:

- **Deep Fried Dog Doo.** Raw materials available at any park.

- **Deep Fried Already-Chewed Gum.** Available under school desks and subway seats.

- **Deep Fried Lint.** Available in most pockets and a host of belly buttons.

- **Deep Fried Shards of Glass.** Available in most vacant lots.

And, lest we forget the vegan and vegetarian crowd,

- **Deep Fried Grass Clippings, Leaves and Twigs.** Available in most gated communities.

Now we're talking! Look for my booth at your local fair. I'll have the one with the really long lines. And with all the big-ass people around, there should be more than enough shade...

CHAPTER 43

LONG BLOGS, TRENCH COATS, AND FAST FOOD RELIGION

I used to write a weekly blog. I enjoyed it and may restart it one day.

However, many folk said that my blog posts are too long.

I got a visit from the blog goons recently. Two burly guys in trench coats and starched white shirts. The one called Mikey Payday (I guess cuz his face looked just like a Payday candy bar) hoisted me up by my collar and threw me against the wall while his colleague, Kit-Kat Johnny (his face also looked like a Payday bar, but they couldn't have two guys named Payday in the same gang so they called him Kit-Kat) waved a freshly-opened bottle of WiteOut® under my nose and seethed, "Your blogs are too long. You're making all the other bloggers look bad. Like they ain't got enough to say. You gotta cut back."

I gulped and sputtered, "Cut back? How much?"

Mikey Payday drew his face close to mine. "Half."

My eyes grew wide. "Half?"

"What is there, an echo in here?"

"Well, sometimes when all the windows are shut and the ceiling fan isn't running you can quite often hear an…"

"Shaddup!" Kit-Kat said as he jabbed a finger into my chest. "In half. By tomorrow. Or else." And with that the two goons spun on their heels and marched out of the room.

I stared down at my blog draft and sighed. In half? But how? Then it hit me. I could delete every other letter! That'd certainly do it! I sat down and feverishly retyped my blog, posted it, then sat back and waited for the comments to roll in. It didn't take long. The first was from my agent.

"What the heck do you call this jibber jabber?"

I tried to explain about the trench coats and the deceptively intoxicating smell of Wite-Out, but she cut me off.

"Good grief, Caterson. Your blog reads like it was typed in tongues by some Pentecostal evangelist!"

I glanced down at my delete-every-other-letter blog. She was right. Heck, I wasn't even a blogger anymore. I was a bogr (which is pronounced 'booger' in some parts of Bavaria). I slammed the phone down and bowed my head in abject failure. Then I heard a knock at the door. The mailman. I opened it and he dumped two duffle bags of express mail at my feet. All filled with prayer requests and checks. And the letters kept coming. For days.

I finally called my agent to tell her that my blogging in tongues had made me a bona fide Blogging Pentecostal Evangelist and that I was only 75 cents short of clearing a gazillion dollars.

"Fantastic," she said, no doubt thinking about her 15 percent cut. "Now there are only two more things you have to do to become the primo Pentecostal Evangelist of the blogosphere."

"What's that?" I asked. "Go to seminary and get ordained?"

"No. You need to bone your secretary and then cry about it on TV."

"You know I can't do that!"

"Why?"

"I don't have a TV."

Then it happened. I lost my following overnight to a new evangelist who claimed he could predict the future for his generous followers. All they had to do is reset all dates and clocks on their computers back 24 hours and he'd predict what would happen to them today. I'm sure it wasn't long 'til the post office was dumping mounds of letters and checks on his doorstep.

Well, my time as a famous internet evangelist was certainly short-lived. And that's probably for the best.

Sometimes I think religion in America is a lot like fast food. We want it convenient, we want it our way, and we want it now. If someone down the street can serve what we want up faster, well, as they say, "See ya, wouldn't want to be ya."

I went to church last week. The service was from the 4th century and lasted nearly two hours. We pretty much stood the whole time. I'm glad I went.

Slow food is good. So is slow religion.

So one day I may get around to writing blogs again. And I'm sorry I've taken up so much of your time reminiscing. But to make it up to you, I've included some killer b'fast recipes. It's not exactly fast food but it won't chew up your entire morning either.

And if you set your computer clock back to yesterday, I'll even predict what you might have for breakfast this morning.

• AIN'T GOT TIME FOR BREAKFAST BREAKFASTS •

I love to make breakfast. Eggs, bacon or sausage, home fries, side of fruit, toast, coffee and orange juice. Problem is, sometimes I just don't have the time to do it. Or sometimes I'm by myself and can't justify the effort to make just one serving. So I turn to these easy options. Try a few. I'm sure you'll return to them often as well.

• BREAD, BAGELS OR ENGLISH MUFFINS •

DIRECTIONS
1. Toast rye or whole wheat bread, bagels or English muffins

2. Then:
   - Top each half with whipped creamed cheese, smoked salmon, slice tomatoes and red onions, and a spoonful of drained capers

   - Top each half with whipped cream cheese and fruit: blueberries, raspberry's, sliced strawberries, bananas, etc. or a combination.

   - Top each half with a scrambled or fried egg, fresh or frozen spinach, sliced tomatoes and shredded mozzarella cheese. Broil in a toaster oven until cheese melts.

   - Top one half with Greek yogurt and fruit: blueberries, sliced strawberries, bananas, etc. or a combination. Place the other half on top to make a sandwich

   - Top one half with sliced ham and grated cheddar cheese. Broil in a toaster oven until cheese melts. Place the other half on top to make a sandwich

   - Top one half with peanut butter, sliced apples and sliced ham. Place the other half on top to make a sandwich

   - Top one half with peanut butter, sliced bananas and crumbled bacon (I often make extra bacon then crumble and freeze it so I always have it on hand.)

   - Top one half with sliced mozzarella cheese, sliced tomatoes, and a spoonful of pesto sauce (jarred is fine for this) Place the other half on top to make a sandwich

• GRITS •

Be sure to use either regular or quick-cooking grits. Avoid instant grits. They lack flavor and texture and the small amount of time saved just isn't worth it.

DIRECTIONS
1. Prepare grits according to the directions on the package.

2. Top each bowl with:

   - 2 fried eggs or poached eggs, a chopped scallion, salsa, and grated cheddar cheese

   - A pat of butter, golden raisins, some brown sugar, and toasted crumbled pecans or walnuts

   - A scoop of ricotta cheese and chopped fresh fruit (strawberries, figs, peaches, etc)

   - Sautéed onions and red peppers and grated Parmesan cheese

   - Canned or fresh chopped tomatoes and grated Parmesan cheese

• EGGS •

EGGS OVER BLACK BEANS: Simmer a half can of black beans and a cup of chicken broth in an omelet pan. Crack two eggs into the mixture and cook until the whites have set. Drizzle with hot sauce.

EGGS AND SALSA: Heat a cup of salsa in an omelet pan. Throw in a handful or two of tortilla chips. Cook until the chips start to soften but still retain some crunch. Top with 2 fried eggs, some sliced onion, grated cheddar cheese and, for a nice touch, a little lime juice.

EGGS AND VEGGIE BREAKFAST IN A CUP: Lightly oil the inside of a microwave-safe 12-ounce coffee cup. Add one egg, 1/4 cup chopped frozen broccoli (defrosted) 1/4 cup chopped mushrooms, and 1 tablespoon water. Stir until blended. Place in a microwave and cook for 30 seconds. Stir and cook until eggs is almost set, about 30 – 45 seconds longer. Top with grated mozzarella cheese.

HAM AND EGGS BREAKFAST IN A CUP: Lightly the inside of a microwave-safe 12-ounce coffee cup. Add one egg, 1/4 cup chopped mushrooms, one slice deli ham torn into shreds, and 1 tablespoon water. Place in a microwave and cook for 30 seconds. Stir and cook until eggs is almost set, about 30 – 45 seconds longer. Top with grated cheddar cheese.

CHAPTER 44

WHO YOU CALLING A SHRIMP? CONFESSIONS FROM A LITTLE GUY

Face it. I was a little guy in elementary school and on through high school. I still am pretty much a little guy. Now it doesn't matter so much. But back in the day it did. I was somewhat limited to what JV or varsity sports I could play. No football or basketball for me. I was even limited to the girls I could date with having to succumb to the social pressure at the time to not date any girl who was taller than you. So I opted for soccer, wrestling and gymnastics where height wasn't a factor. But rather than moan about my limitations, me and some like minded and equally altitudinally-challenged friends created our own clique known as 'The Little People'. We ate lunch together, hung out in the halls together, and played sports together. We even had our own 'handshake' – we'd 'slap each other five' with just our pinkies while squealing 'nee-nee-nee-nee'. Some of The Little People excelled at sports, some aced every exam they took, and some of us were very funny, which earned us the title of class clowns. Bottom line? We made the best out of what God had made us.

My cousin-in-law was equally altitudinally-challenged but he took a different tact. He wasn't into sports or academia. Instead, He appeared in class plays and – gasp – took dance lessons, which was unheard of for guys in my day. While I'm sure he had to endure much ridicule from larger and more traditionally athletic young men, he went on to marry my cousin (a fellow dance class student) and went on to a stellar career on Broadway where he was in the original cast of *A Chorus Line*, appeared with Liza Minnelli in *New York, New York*, and more recently choreographed Molly Ringwald in *Sweet Chastity* before going on to stage the Broadway mega-hit *Wicked*.

Not too bad for a little guy from Mamaroneck, New York.

My only regret? I didn't take up cooking until later in life. Had I done so earlier, I might've avoided a lot of sore muscles and bruises, yet still would've garnered the admiration of my peers. Hey, everyone is drawn to and admires someone who can prepare a good meal. Especially those of the opposite sex.

That's why I enjoy teaching others how to cook. Especially simple and easy-to-prepare meals using readily available ingredients. I love doing it on stage at large festivals and for smaller audiences at local libraries or community centers. But one of my favorites? Doing cooking classes for tweens and teens. Face it, many kids won't learn how to cook because their parents don't.

So when I'm doing classes and presentations for tweens and teens, I always share with them the benefits of learning how to cook:

a.   You'll eat healthier because you control the ingredients.

b.   You'll have more money in your pocket 'cuz cooking at home is cheaper than eating out

c.   You'll become very popular because not many people can cook well nowadays.

So even if you're short like me, it won't keep you from making these wonderfully delicious recipes that are short in ingredients. Especially if you're short on time. So lemme see those pinkies and slap me five with a 'nee-nee-nee-nee'.

• SAUTEÉD CAJUN SHRIMP •

PREP: 5 minutes   MARINATE: 10+ minutes

COOK: 8 minutes

INGREDIENTS

3/4 pound large or extra large shrimp, peeled and deveined

3/4 teaspoon smoked or sweet paprika

1/2 teaspoon thyme

1/2 teaspoon oregano

1/8 teaspoon cayenne pepper or more to taste

1/4 teaspoon salt or more to taste

1/4 teaspoon fresh ground pepper, or more to taste

1 tablespoon unsalted butter

1 tablespoon olive or canola oil

1 clove garlic, minced or pressed

DIRECTIONS

1. In medium bowl, combine the paprika, thyme, oregano, cayenne pepper, salt, pepper and black pepper. Add the shrimp and toss to coat. Allow to sit for at least 10 minutes or up to 1/2 hour.

2. In the meantime, heat a 10-inch skillet over medium-high heat. Add the butter and oil and swirl to coat. Add the garlic and sauté until fragrant, about 1 minute. Add the shrimp are pink but still tender, about 4 or 5 minutes.

Serve with steamed white rice or dirty rice.

• SAUTEÉD SPANISH SHRIMP •
(Gambas al Ajillo)

PREP: 5 minutes   COOK: 8 minutes

INGREDIENTS

   3 tablespoons extra virgin olive oil cup olive

   2 cloves garlic, minced or pressed

   3/4 pound large or extra large shrimp, peeled and deveined

   1/2 teaspoon smoked paprika

   1/2 teaspoon ground cumin

   Pinch of saffron

   Kosher salt and fresh ground pepper to taste

   Chopped fresh parsley to garnish

DIRECTIONS

1. In medium bowl, combine the paprika, cumin, salt, pepper and black pepper. Add the shrimp and toss to coat. Allow to sit for at least 5 minutes or up to 1/2 hour.

2. Meanwhile, heat a 10-inch skillet over medium-high heat. Add the olive oil and swirl to coat. Add the garlic and sauté until fragrant, about 1 – 2 minutes. Add the shrimp and sauté until pink but still tender, about 4 – 5 minutes.

Serve over steamed white rice.

• GREEK SAUTEÉD SHRIMP •

PREP: 5 minutes   COOK: 8 minutes

INGREDIENTS
  3/4 pound large or extra large shrimp, peeled and deveined shrimp
  1 tablespoon unsalted butter
  1 tablespoons olive oil
  2 garlic cloves, minced, or pressed
  1/4 teaspoon chili powder
  2 tablespoons chopped Italian flat leaf parsley
  1-1/2 tablespoons fresh lemon juice
  1/4 teaspoon kosher salt, or more to taste
  1/2 cup crumbled feta cheese (about 2 - 3 ounces)

DIRECTIONS
  1.   Heat a 10-inch skillet over medium-high heat. Add the olive oil and swirl to
       coat. Add the garlic chili powder and sauté until fragrant, about
       1 – 2 minutes.

  2.   Add the shrimp and sauté until pink but still tender, about 4 – 5 minutes.
       Stir in the parsley, lemon juice and salt. Sprinkle with feta cheese and let
       melt a little.

Serve over orzo.

• ITALIAN SAUTEÉD SHRIMP •

PREP: 5 minutes   COOK: 8 minutes

INGREDIENTS
  3/4 pound large or extra large shrimp, peeled and deveined
  1/4 cup extra virgin olive oil or 4 tablespoons unsalted butter, divided
  3 garlic cloves, minced or pressed
  2 roma tomatoes, chopped
  2 teaspoons tomato paste
  2 teaspoons white wine vinegar
  1/4 cup chicken broth
  1/4 teaspoon Italian herb seasoning (or more to taste)
  1/4 teaspoon kosher salt (or more to taste)
  Juice of from 3 fresh lemon slices
  Chopped fresh Italian flat leaf parsley to garnish

DIRECTIONS
1.   Heat a 10-inch skillet over medium-high heat. Add half the oil or butter and swirl to coat. Add the shrimp and sauté until pink but still tender, about 4 – 5 minutes. Pour shrimp into a bowl to reserve.

2.   Add the remaining oil and butter to the skillet and swirl to coat. Add the garlic and sauté until fragrant, about 1 – 2 minutes Add chopped roma tomatoes and cook until soft, about 4 – 6 minutes.

3.   Meanwhile, in a small bowl, combine the tomato past, vinegar, broth, Italian herbs and salt then stir into the tomatoes. Bring to boil then reduce to medium-low. Simmer, until it is reduced by half, about 4-6 minutes, stirring occasionally.

4.   Add shrimp back to skillet and toss in sauce to combine. Garnish with chopped fresh parsley.

Serve over orzo.

CHAPTER 45

WHY YOU SHOULD NEVER BUY KITCHEN GEAR
AT A FLEA MARKET OR CARNIVAL

When I was a college student back the 70's, my girlfriend and I would occasionally visit the local flea market. Heck, it was a cheap and entertaining Sunday afternoon diversion for two broke college kids.

One afternoon we stumbled into a crowd of people entranced by a man standing on a stage built from 2 by 4's and plywood. A few red-ripe tomatoes, empty Coca-Cola cans, and a Chuck Taylor Converse Sneaker rested on the table in front of him.

He was dazzling the crowd with his well-rehearsed patter about a new, revolutionary knife from the Orient. 100% surgical stainless steel. Micro-serrated. Ergonomic handle.

Oh. And dishwasher safe.

He boasted that this wonder would cut through a ripe tomato as though it was warm butter, and then eased the blade through a bright red beefsteak. Then he picked up the soda can and announced that the very same knife would slice through aluminum just as easily. And he did. The crowed gasped in delight. Then he grabbed the Chuck Taylor and sliced it. Those gathered broke out into a raucous applause that only a flea market could elicit from folks who'd spent the previous night at the local roadhouse downing Milwaukee's Best, Boone's Farm sangria, and rum with generic labels.

"I bet your knife can't do that!" he said as the applause died out. "It even comes with a lifetime warrantee – it'll be as sharp in twenty years as it is the day you buy it."

He went on to say that a Ginzu knife like this would cost $19.95 in stores, but those of us who were lucky enough to come to the flea market could buy it for just $10.

He sold them as fast as his pretty assistant could yank them out of cardboard boxes.

I was one of them.

At the time, I didn't even cook. It was going to be a mother's day present. My girlfriend was a little less enthused.

"Shouldn't you wait? Read up on it? Go down to the library and see what Consumer Reports says or something?" Remember, this was before Al Gore invented the Internet so nothing could be Googled.

"Why?" I said as I fished a ten-dollar bill out of my wallet. "It's got a lifetime warrantee! If it doesn't work I'll just bring it back. What's to lose?"

She shrugged her shoulders and smirked.

We stopped at a grocery store on the way home and I bought two plump tomatoes and a six-pack of Dr. Pepper. That night I gathered my friends in my dorm room and amazed them as I sliced through a tomato then through an empty Dr. Pepper. I wanted a sneaker, but I didn't want to use one of mine and my friends didn't want to give theirs up. So I sawed through another tomato and can. I was on a roll. Basking in the 'ooh's and ahh's'.

But when I tried the tomato a third time it didn't slice like a hot knife through butter. In fact, it didn't slice at all. I examined the knife – the serrated edges were bent. Dull beyond belief.

My girlfriend got that 'I told you so' smirk again.

"Not to worry," I said as I placed the knife back in the box. "It has a lifetime warranty. I'll just get my money back."

The next day I looked for paperwork that may have come in box. There wasn't any. Nada. Even the box lacked a company address or phone number. Oh well, I thought. I'll just go back to the flea market and get my money back.

The next Sunday I headed to the market with my smirking girlfriend in tow. I searched the grounds for the knife salesman. He was nowhere to be found. I did, however, notice quite a few people making the rounds with a box similar to the one clutched in my hand. They all seemed pretty steamed about something. Perhaps they too had a sliced tomato or two, a few soda cans, and even maybe an old sneaker only to find their knives as dull as their Aunt Millie's vacation slides.

Me? I just chalked it up to a nineteen-year-old kid who had $10 burning a hole in his pocket and got sucked into the 'next best thing'.

But all wasn't lost.

I still gave the knife to my mom. Heck, I was stone-broke and couldn't afford another gift. She accepted it with love. And even though my mom could never use the ruined knife as it was intended, it did serve a purpose.

She discovered that the thin, flexible blade popped open the bolt on the door from the garage to the house. So when she locked herself out, the ginzu knife would get her back in. It was more effective than a credit card and it didn't chew up the doorjamb like a screwdriver. Eventually the knife found its way to a hook next to the door in the garage where it hangs to this day.

I still remember times when I'd show up unexpectedly with friends or my family in tow only to find myself locked out. We'd head into the garage and I'd snatch the knife off the hook. They'd always stare and ask, "What the heck is that?"

"It's a door opener."

"I never saw one like that."

"It's Oriental."

"Man, those Japanese got it going on with the tech thing."

"You have no idea."

Then, after a jiggle or two, we were in.

My lesson? If something is too good to be true, it probably is. I also learned that you don't always get what you pay for; remember, I bought that $10 knife when the minimum wage was less than $2 bucks an hour. That knife today would probably hover around $40.

Not exactly cheap.

But neither are good chef's knives. An 8-inch or 10-inch chef's knife from a great company like Wüstof or Zwilling J. A. Henkels will set you back around $135 to $150.

That may sound like a lot for a kitchen tool, but remember, a good chef's knife will work wonders in your kitchen. It'll do everything a food processor or other fancy chopping gadget will do. Plus, with care, it'll last you your lifetime, your kid's lifetime, and your grandkid's lifetime.

Looking at it like that, it's not a bad investment (I own both Wüstof and Henkels chef's knives).

I'm going to let you in on a hint. I buy a lot of my kitchen gear at places like Home Goods, Marshalls, TJ Maxx, Tuesday Morning, etc. One time I was in Marshalls and they had five Henkels chef's knives marked down from $139.95 to $35.95. I bought all five. I kept one for myself and I gave the others away as Christmas gifts. But first I peeled off the $35.95 price tag and left on the $139.95 price tag. I know. I'm bad. But I tell you what. I started receiving much better gifts from my friends after that.

Unfortunately, you just can't walk into those places with a list of things you want. You have to buy what they have. I haven't seen a similar deal on knives since that day almost a decade ago. So here's some tips you can use right now.

First off, if you're buying knives, don't immediately gravitate toward those big block sets with a gazillion knives (a mediocre one will set you back $100 bucks and good one will set you back anywhere from $500 to over $2,000 bucks).

You don't need all those knives. In fact, you really just need three to do most of the heavy lifting in your kitchen.

Yep, three.

Write this down:

- An 8-inch or 10-inch chef's knife

- A 3-1/4-inch to 4-inch paring knife

- A 10-inch serrated bread knife

Surprised? Most chefs will tell you the same thing.

A chef's knife is the kitchen workhorse. It'll slice, dice, mince, and chop like nobody's business. And like I said above, it'll set you back $135 to $150 bucks.

A paring knife will take care of the little stuff. That'll run around $50.

A serrated knife will cut bread, tomatoes and other delicate items. Cost? About $100 bucks.

That's $300 bucks, more or less, for three mandatory knives. Still a lot cheaper than buying a big block set.

But since most of us are on a budget, I'm going to recommend knives that are not only some of the world's best, but are also the most affordable. (Don't just take my word for it, Cook's Illustrated and Consumer Reports and other reputable reviewers agree).

So let's buy good ones at a price that won't break the bank.

The key word is a company called Forschner and their knives are called Victorinox. Never heard of them? Neither did I until about 20 years ago. But heck, these folk have been producing Swiss Army Knives since forever. I know you've heard of Swiss Army Knives.

As of this writing, a three piece set on Amazon that includes an 8-inch chef's knife, 3.25-inch paring knife and a 10.25-inch bread knife will cost you under $90. You can't go wrong with that.

Just promise me that you'll never put any of your good knives through the dishwasher. They'll get banged up and dull that way. Always hand-wash and let them air dry. You'll get a lot more mileage out of them.

Now go grab that serrated bread knife. We're going to put it to the test on some fresh vine-ripe tomatoes.

• BROILED TOMATOES WITH PARMESAN CHEESE •

Here's another easy dish that's ready for some improv. Simply substitute the parmesan cheese with an equal amount of mozzarella, feta, or bagged Italian four cheese mix. Feel free to increase the amount of cheese if you prefer a cheesier finish.

PREP: 5 minutes   COOK: Under 5 minutes

INGREDIENTS
    2 ripe tomatoes, cut into 1/4-inch slices
    2 tablespoons extra virgin olive oil
    1/2 teaspoon kosher salt
    1/2 teaspoon ground black pepper, or to taste
    2 cloves garlic, minced or pressed
    1-1/2 tablespoons chopped fresh oregano or 2 teaspoon dried.
    6 tablespoons freshly grated Parmesan cheese

DIRECTIONS
1. Preheat broiler. Cover a broiler pan or baking sheet with parchment paper or aluminum foil (I really like using parchment paper), and mist with non-stick cooking spray or olive oil.

2. Arrange tomato slices in a single layer on the prepared baking sheet. Drizzle each slice lightly with olive oil, spreading oil evenly with your finger. Season with salt, pepper, garlic, and oregano. Sprinkle Parmesan cheese over the top.

3. Broil, 3 inches from the heat until cheese is browned and bubbly, about 3 minutes.

CHAPTER 46

A MYTH ITH ATH GOOD ATH A MILE

Thorry.

I tharted to write thith chapter after eating a huge peanut butter thandwich. Hold on. Let me wath it down with thomething.

There. That's better.

Over the past few chapters, we've shared some great kitchen tips and hints and had a few laughs while we were at it. But in discussing these great pearls of culinary wisdom, I came to realize that among the real pearls there exist more than a few shams. But because they're repeated so often, people begin to accept them as true. Sorta like your congressman telling you that he is "only there to help", or your dentist telling you "this won't hurt a bit", or your crazy uncle Larry telling you to relax 'cuz "he's done this a million times and it's never got him arrested" (Not counting last Friday night in Biloxi which he assures you was an honest-to-God fluke).

So I've put together a list of a few bogus kitchen hints and sham pearls of wisdom that would best be left in the back of that drawer in the kitchen where we keep all the crap that doesn't belong in any of the other drawers (Oh, come on. I know you have one of "those" drawers. We all do.)

If you want to reduce the heat of a hot pepper, remove the seeds.
This sham pearl of wisdom is found in more than a few cookbooks but here's the real deal: capsaicin, the substance responsible for the pepper's "heat", is found in the white or pale veins inside the pepper; the seeds themselves contain little or no capsaicin at all. So why do the seeds sometimes taste hot? Because when we slice the peppers, the capsaicin in the veins squirts onto the seeds. So, yeah, ditch the seeds 'cause they might've come in contact with the hot stuff, but to really cut down on the heat, remove the veins.

To prevent pasta from sticking together, add salt or oil to the boiling water.
Interesting concepts, but they won't solve the problem of clumping pasta. Sure, go ahead and add a couple of teaspoons of salt. But only do it for added flavor because it won't help the sticky pasta problem. As for adding the oil? Well, that's only good for wasting oil. The only tried and true way to keep your pasta from sticking together is to use plenty of boiling water and stir the pot occasionally.

Put a box of baking soda in the fridge to absorb odors.

Nope. Putting a box of baking soda in the fridge will just take up more space. While a box of baking soda has the potential to absorb acidic odors, it won't do so effectively because the surface will crust over as it comes in contact with the moist air of the fridge. You'd be better off using the more effective (and expensive) canister of activated charcoal. The simplest and most effective way to control odors in the fridge? Get off your butt and clean it every now and then and be sure to wrap your food up well.

Sushi means "raw fish."

Actually, sushi refers to the rice used in sushi meals. This rice is made by dissolving sugar in vinegar then tossing it with hot rice before serving with other ingredients which may or may not include fish, raw or otherwise. Raw fish, when served by itself, is called sashimi. Unless of course you live in some parts of the deep south where raw fish is often called "bait".

Searing meat seals in the juices.

Not so according to the experts who have the time to test such things. Searing (or browning) meat does create a number of new flavor elements due to what's known as the Maillard Reaction – the denatured proteins recombine with the sugars present to create a deep, more "meaty" flavor, but it won't seal in any juices (as anyone who has grilled a steak and had to deal with flare-ups can assure you.) Sure, some cooks challenge this, and stand by the fact that searing does seal the meat. Me? I side with Harold McGee, the uber-foodie scientist who believes that searing/browning adds great flavor but does little to seal in the juices.

Alcohol burns off when you cook it, so feel free to add another goblet of wine to that stew.

I'm amazed that this idea can still be found in contemporary cookbooks. Alcohol may burn off to some degree, but never entirely. A study by a team of researchers at the University of Idaho, Washington State University, and the US Department of Agriculture's Nutrient Data Laboratory calculated the percentage of alcohol remaining in a dish based on various cooking methods. Here are the results:

- alcohol added to boiling liquid & removed from heat - 85% alcohol retained

- alcohol flamed - 75% alcohol retained

- no heat, stored overnight - 70% alcohol retained

- baked, 25 minutes, alcohol not stirred into mixture - 45% alcohol retained

- baked/simmered, alcohol stirred into mixture:

- 15 minutes - 40% alcohol retained

- 30 minutes - 35% alcohol retained

- 1 hour - 25% alcohol retained

- 1-1/2 hours - 20% alcohol retained

- 2 hours 10% alcohol retained

- 2-1/2 hours 5% alcohol retained.

Bottom line? If you or someone in your household is dealing with the disease of alcoholism, of if you abstain for religious or moral reasons, cooking with wine or other alcoholic beverages is probably not a good idea. Best to use non-alcoholic wine or beef, chicken or vegetable stock. Anything but plain water. Or you can use apple juice in place of white wine and grape or prune juice in place of red. Just be sure to add a little vinegar or lemon juice to offset some of the sweetness.

By the way, if you've sworn off alcohol and don't know what to do with those six bottles of cab in the cupboard, the two Stolis under the sink, and the case of Scotch out in the garage, you got my e-mail (It's not for me. It's for a friend...)

And last but not least:

Most cookbook authors (including myself) always know what they are talking about so you never need to double-check their recommendations for any untruths or moostakes. Oops. I mean mistakes.

Got any myths you'd like to share? Drop me a line!

CHAPTER 47

I LOVE VICTORIA'S SECRET, FRAN LEBOWITZ, AND FEIJOADA. BUT NOT IN THAT ORDER

I got my latest edition of the Victoria's Secret catalog in the mail. For the life of me, I don't know why they keep sending me this stuff. Sheesh, I haven't bought anything from them in over a year and I haven't worn any of their items in the last six months. However, I'm disappointed over the fact that I haven't gotten an invitation to a soirée from Fran Lebowitz lately.

Several of my friends say I should have my head examined. "You're upset about getting Victoria Secret catalogs but you're depressed that you haven't received an invite from Lebowitz? What gives?"

Here's what gives. I admit, the Victoria's Secret models are beautiful. Stunningly so. But the pix have no soul. No depth. And even though Fran Lebowitz has been recognized by Vanity Fair as one of their Best Dressed Women, I doubt she would ever grace the pages of Victoria's Secret.

But given a choice to sit with her and others like her, (the late Dorothy Parker comes to mind), around a resurrected Algonquin Round Table; or with a couple of models from the Spring issue of VS at a corner table in the Rose Bar…well, I'd cast my lot with the likes of Fran and Dorothy. Someone once said that beauty is only skin deep. That may be true. But wit, wisdom and the beauty of one's soul run deeper. And while I'm not one to avert my gaze as a gorgeous woman passes by, there's something winsome, earthy and simple in the writings of women like Fran Lebowitz that is remarkably attractive.

And how does Feijoada (pronounced: fay-ZWAH-da) fit into the equation? Easy. I'm also drawn to dishes that are winsome, earthy and simple. Dishes that have delighted both humble families and self-important monarchs. This Brazilian black bean dish is one such dish. Depth, history, comfort, and spice. It's all there. And there are as many recipes for this as there are cooks. I cooked up a batch for 80+ people who dropped by the house this past Sunday. I've included it here. Scaled down, of course.

Now you'll have to excuse me. My cab just pulled up to take me to West 44th Street for a delicious lunch and scintillating conversation with a cadre of writers, illustrators and journalists – and more than one delightful ghost.

• BRAZILIAN BLACK BEAN SOUP •

(Feijoada)

PREP: 20 minutes   COOK: 2-1/2 hours

INGREDIENTS

1-1/4 cup dried black beans (soaked according to directions on bag)

2 teaspoons olive oil

1/2 pound spicy Italian sausage

1/2 pound pork or beef ribs, trimmed of fat

1/2 cup beef stock

3 cups water

1 small smoke ham hock

1 medium onion, sliced (about 1/2 cup)

1 green pepper, sliced

1 clove garlic, crushed or minced

1/2 teaspoon dried oregano

1/4 teaspoon cumin

1 bay leaf

Kosher salt and freshly ground pepper to taste

1/2 cup diced tomatoes

1/3 cup dry red wine

1 orange, peeled and sectioned

Orange zest and fresh chopped parsley to garnish

DIRECTIONS

1. Heat olive oil in a 10-inch skillet over medium-high heat. Add sausages and ribs and sauté until brown. Remove meat and reserve fat.

2. Add the onions, peppers, garlic, oregano, cumin, and bay leaf to the skillet. Sauté over medium-low heat until onions are soft and translucent, about 8 - 10 minutes. Place vegetable mixture a medium dutch oven or other soup pot.

3. Drain the beans and place in the dutch oven. Add the beef stock, water and meats. Bring to a boil, then partially cover the pot and simmer until the beans are soft, about 1 to 1-1/2 hours, stirring occasionally. Remove the ham hock and ribs and pick away meat. (Cut meat up if necessary). Return meat to the soup.

4. Add the tomatoes and orange slices and continue to simmer for 30 more minutes. Taste for salt and pepper then serve in warm bowls. Garnish with orange zest and fresh parsley.

CHAPTER 48

IF IT AIN'T BROKE, DON'T FIX IT

I was on stage a few years ago at the Georgia Wild Shrimp & Grits Festival in Jekyll Island, Georgia. Let me tell you, this is a wonderful event. Why? The location (on the grounds of the historic Jekyll Island Hotel) is magnificent. So is the staff and everyone who attends.

Yes, ambiance, history, great folks, and a gentle sea breeze wafting through the trees made for a delightful day. In fact, it's usually so delightful, many attendees come for the whole weekend.

Of course, the centerpiece culinary-wise, is the shrimp & grits. Hundreds line up to savor this low country dish prepared by pros and amateurs alike as part of a grueling cooking competition. Heck, they even bring in a few celebrity chefs who show you how it's done on the Cooking Stage. (Yeah, that was me up there clad in the very non-South Georgian Caribbean shirt, baggy cotton beach pants, and Jimmy Buffett flip-flops).

But here I must offer a caveat.

I'm from New York. Born and raised just outside the city. Then my parents moved to Tampa Bay where I finished high school. I then attended college down near Miami before drifting back up to Tampa Bay to get married and start a family.

Why am I telling you this? Because grits were about as common in my dietary regimen as ham hocks would be at the annual pot luck at the Beth Emeth Synagogue down on the Boston Post Road in Larchmont.

When I finally moved to Chattanooga (the real south) in the late eighties, I had my first sampling of grits. As a cook and connoisseur of all things food, I felt I needed to give them a try. Needless to say, I was underwhelmed.

Oh, they didn't taste bad. Bad had nothing to do with it. It was the taste that was lacking.

Perhaps you've never had grits. If so, let me describe them for you. Did you ever work with papier-mâché when you were a kid? Did you ever eat any of the goop before you dipped the newspaper into it? Of course you did. We all did.

Grits are a lot like that. Except grittier.

So imagine throwing a couple of handfuls of sand into your papier-mâché goop before tasting it. Yeah. That about sums up grits.

But wait! I hear the southerners chiming in: You need to add salt! (Evidently lots of salt.) And grated cheese! (Gobs of cheese.) And butter! (One stick or two?) That way, the lowly grits will rise in your culinary estimation. Of course, with a couple of tablespoons of salt, a cup or two of grated cheese and a stick of butter, even a carburetor would taste good.

So I decided to stick with the oh-so-dependable (and tasty) home fries sautéed in onions and peppers for my breakfast. Or any other time when grits might be an option.

Until I tried Shrimp & Grits.

Now I'm a bona fide grits fan. Maybe it was the shrimp that did it. Who knows? But now I'm a fan.

And here's the interesting thing. There aren't a lot of variations with this dish (as there are for chili, marinara sauce, beef stew, etc.) Why? Because it's good from the get-go. So if it ain't broke, don't fix it.

But being a wise-ass chef, I had to try and "fix it".

So while I didn't change the basics, I did make a few minor alterations. I cooked my shrimp with the grits then made a shrimp gravy to serve over them. And according to the crowd who sampled it at the Festival, it was a winner.

So go ahead and give this a shot, even if you're from the Bronx. And if your lover tells you that they don't eat grits, heck, tell 'em it's papier-mâché. They'll love you for it!

• SHRIMP AND GRITS - MY WAY •

PREP: 5 minutes   COOK: 30 minutes

INGREDIENTS

3/4 pound large shrimp, peeled and de-veined

1 tablespoon olive or canola oil

1 clove garlic, crushed or minced

Pinch of cayenne pepper

3/4 teaspoon kosher salt (use less if your bacon is very salty), divided

1/2 teaspoon freshly ground pepper, divided

2 slices bacon, chopped

1 small onion, finely chopped (about 1/2 cup)

1-1/2 cups water

1/2 cup heavy cream

1/2 teaspoon hot sauce, or to taste (Frank's or Huy Fong's Sriracha is fine)

1/2 cup quick-cook grits (not instant)

4 ounces good extra-sharp cheddar cheese, grated (about 1 cup)

2 or 3 scallions, green part only, sliced for garnish

DIRECTIONS

1. Preheat oven to 375°. Toss the shrimp with the oil, garlic, cayenne pepper, 1/4 teaspoon salt and 1/8 teaspoon pepper in a small bowl. Refrigerate while preparing the grits.

2. Sauté the bacon in a 10-inch skillet over medium heat until crisp, about 8 - 10 minutes. Remove bacon with a slotted spoon and place on a paper towel-lined plate to drain. Add onions and sauté until soft and translucent. About 5 - 7 minutes.

3. Stir in the water, cream, hot sauce, and remaining salt and pepper and bring to a boil. Slowly stir in the grits, reduce the heat to low and cook, stirring often, until the grits are thick and creamy, about 5 - 8 minutes.

4. Remove from heat and stir in the grated cheese. Remove shrimp from the fridge and place on top of the grits in a circle, pressing on each one until they're buried about half-way. Place in the oven and bake until shrimp are cooked through, about 5 - 8 minutes depending on the size of the shrimp. (Or you may add the shrimp to the skillet and cook over medium, stirring, until shrimp are pink and cooked through.)

Ladle shrimp gravy (below) over all and sprinkle with chopped scallions and bacon bits.

• SHRIMP GRAVY •

PREP: 5 minutes   COOK: 30 minutes

INGREDIENTS
   1 slice bacon, chopped
   1/4 cup minced onion
   1/2 cup diced red bell pepper
   1/4 cup diced celery
   1/2 pound large shrimp, coarsely chopped
   1/2 teaspoon kosher salt
   1/8 teaspoon freshly ground pepper
   pinch dried red pepper or to taste
   1/2 cup shrimp, chicken, or vegetable broth
   1/2 teaspoon browning sauce (Kitchen Bouquet is fine)

DIRECTIONS
   1. Sauté the bacon in a 10-inch skillet over medium heat until crisp and brown,
       about 8 - 10 minutes. Remove bacon with a slotted spoon and place on a
       paper towel-lined plate to drain.

   2. Add the onion, red pepper and celery and sauté until tender, about 8 - 10
       minutes. Add the shrimp and sauté until they turn pink and opaque, about 2 -
       3 more minutes.

   3. Remove shrimp and vegetables with a slotted spoon and reserve in a bowl.
       Add the broth and browning sauce to the skillet. Season with salt, pepper
       and dried red pepper. Bring to a boil then simmer for 1 - 2 minutes. Return
       the shrimp, vegetables and bacon to the sauce and heat for 1 more minute.
       Serve over shrimp & grits.

CHAPTER 49

WOK AND WOLL – DINING ON THE RITZ WHEN YOUR WALLET'S ON THE FRITZ

We've all been there. More bills due at the end of the month than there is in the checking account. But need we sacrifice our dining experience because we lack the cash? Of course we could always turn to our trusty ramen noodles (see Chapter 15) but what if we want something more substantial. Or something we'd be proud to serve our boyfriend or girlfriend, in-laws, boss, or anyone else we might want to impress?

Then it just might be time to wok and woll.

By that, I mean stir-fry. The nearly ubiquitous method for whipping up a healthy, inexpensive, and lightning-quick dish that will please the most discriminating palate. Widely employed in China for millennia, preparing food in a bit of hot oil in a pan known as a wok has become a mainstay in countries throughout the world. The Chinese word for this method of cooking is chao, and is translated as stir-fry in English. I think that pretty well describes it.

And here's the real beauty of it. You won't need to run out and buy a lot of new equipment to prepare a delicious stir-fry. In fact, I would counsel you not to. You probably already have the necessary gear to create any number of stir-fry dishes right now. But wait, you say, I don't have a wok! Or as many folks put it, 'a wok pan'. (Which is sort of redundant. It'd be like saying 'auto car' as in "Dad, can I borrow the keys to the auto car tonight?")

But I digress.

Here's why you don't have to run out and buy a wok. (And if you already have one, why you shouldn't use it). The traditional round-bottomed wok was meant to be used over a hot flame that enveloped the pan creating a variety of cooking surfaces from searing hot in the center, to not so searing hot up the sides. Traditional woks like these were not designed for flat-topped stoves. And if you use the 'ring' that accompanies it, the pan will be too far above the source of heat to be really effective. Some manufacturers addressed this by creating woks with flat-bottoms so they wouldn't wobble all over the stove. The problem with this solution is that the typical cooking surface on a flat-bottomed wok is only 6 – 7 inches; a lot less than a 12-inch skillet.

So if you have a 10 or 12-inch skillet (either cast iron, non-stick, tri-ply) you have the basic pan to create a great stir-fry. An added bonus? As you know, woks are really big. Do you really have the space in your kitchen to add yet another item that you'll use only occasionally? I don't. The other consideration is maintenance. A good wok will be carbon steel and will require seasoning and regular upkeep. I already spend time doing that with my cast iron skillet. Do I really need another item that needs babysitting in my kitchen? Nope.

Now that we have the wok thing out of the way, does one need to invest in specially designed wok spatulas and ladles? Once again, nope. While a traditional Chinese restaurant with a line of huge and properly seated woks might need spatulas and ladles with 17-inch or 18-inch handles, that's a bit overkill for me. It'd look down right silly for me to use something as long as a canoe paddle in my tiny kitchen. Restaurants need them because their woks are huge and blazing hot and chefs need to keep their distance. For the likes of you and I, a couple of good spatulas (wood, bamboo, silicon, metal) will do just fine. Same with the ladles.

Now let's move onto some basics before we launch into a few great recipes:

1. Pre-heat the pan and cook over lots of heat. If you don't, you'll just wind up steaming or braising your meat and veggies.

2. Cut everything into small and even-sized pieces so they cook quickly.

3. Have everything ready before you start. Stir-frying is very quick. You won't have time to julienne those carrots while the onions are cooking.

4. Make sure you pat your meat, poultry or seafood dry so that it sears and doesn't steam in its own moisture.

5. Stir-fry your meat, chicken or seafood first and remove it to a plate when it's about 80 per cent done. Stir-fry your veggies then add the meat back in for the final cooking.

6. Stir-fry onions first, then add hard veggies like carrots, broccoli or water chestnuts. Quicker cooking veggies like garlic, snow peas, leafy greens, tomatoes, bean sprouts or bamboo shoots should be added towards the end of cooking.

7. Add your sauce and pre-cooked noodles last. You just want to heat them though.

8. Keep things moving! The purpose of a stir-fry is to cook things quickly. This is not the time to check your emails or text a friend.

Now that we have the basics down. Let's make a stir-fry. In keeping with the theme of this book, I'm going to show you a basic lo mein recipe that you can tweak to your heart's content. Once you commit it to memory, you'll be able to toss together a beef, pork, chicken, lamb, fish, shrimp or veggie dish in no time.

And yes, it'll be good enough for the boss and his wife.

• NO MUSS, NO FUSS LO MEIN •

This is great for several reasons: you can cook just about any protein, with a wide range of veggies, in one pan, in a matter of minutes. Feel free to pick up real lo mein noodles in the oriental section of the supermarket. Me? I just use regular spaghetti, linguini or fettuccini because I always have it on hand and it's dirt cheap if you get it BOGO.

PREP: 10 minutes   COOK: 10 minutes

INGREDIENTS
    1/4 pound beef, chicken, pork, fish, shrimp, or firm tofu diced

    1 tablespoon soy sauce

    1 tablespoon sherry

    1 tablespoon vegetable or peanut oil, divided

    1 small onion, peeled and halved from pole to pole, then cut into wedges

    1 clove garlic, minced or pressed

    1-1/2 teaspoons minced ginger

    1/4 pound veggies, diced

    Basic Chao Sauce (see below)

    2 cups cooked spaghetti (about 4 ounces uncooked)

FOR THE CHAO SAUCE

In a small bowl, mix together:

    2 tablespoons chicken broth

    2 tablespoons soy sauce

    1 teaspoon rice wine vinegar (or white wine vinegar)

    1 teaspoon sesame oil

    1/2 teaspoon red pepper flakes

    1/2 teaspoon sugar

DIRECTIONS

1. Prepare pasta according to directions (or use leftover pasta).

2. In a medium bowl, combine the beef, poultry, pork or seafood with the soy sauce and sherry. Toss to coat. Organize the onion, veggies, garlic and ginger on a large plate or small bowls so they're ready to go.

3. Heat a 10 or 12-inch skillet over medium-high heat. Add half the oil and swirl to coat. Remove the protein from the marinade and pat dry. Add the onion to the skillet and stir-fry until lightly brown, but still crisp, about 1 minute. Add the beef, chicken, pork or seafood to the skillet and sauté until seared and just barely cooked, about 2 – 3 minutes (a little less for the seafood). Remove to a bowl and cover to keep warm.

4. If using two types of veggies (one hard and one soft) add the hard veggies and stir-fry until lightly cooked and crisp, about 1 – 2 minutes. Add the soft veggies and stir-fry for 1 – 2 minutes. Add the garlic and ginger and stir-fry for 1 minute.

5. Transfer the veggies to the bowl with the meat. Add the remaining oil to the skillet and swirl to coat. When it just begins to shimmer, add the spaghetti and toss until heated through, about 2 minutes. Return the meat and veggies to the skillet and add the Chao Sauce. Toss to combine until heated through.

CHAPTER 50

THE SECRET'S IN THE SAUCE

While the term 'the secret's in the sauce' found it's way into the nation's vocabulary through the award-winning film *Fried Green Tomatoes*, no one really knows the true origin of it. But we do know it's been used by all manner of chefs and cooks since forever even if they weren't referring to barbecue created from the remains of an accused wife beater.

The phrase even found its way out of the kitchen and has become an idiom that's often used whenever someone acknowledges a job-well-done and asks how such a great feat was accomplished or how a great product was made. To keep things proprietary, the creator may reply (often with a 'wink, wink') that the secret's in the sauce.

In this chapter I'm taking the phrase back into the kitchen where it belongs.

We're going to learn to create a few pan sauces that'll transform your basic sautéed beef, chicken and pork into something marvelous.

And when your guests rave over your creation and pester you with questions about how you made a pedestrian piece of chicken like the breast into a mouth-watering entrée, you can just smile and…well…you'll know what to say.

We're also going to learn to make a perfect, yet oh-so-simple, balsamic vinaigrette, several ways to amp us bottled barbeque sauce, and a simple sauce that'll transform just about any dessert.

First we're going to start off with a basic sauté and pan sauce. And when I say basic, I mean basic. No intense use of spices, no marinating, no exotic vegetables. We'll save those for another book. I just want you to see simple it is to turn a basic meat, poultry or seafood dish into something extraordinary by simply whipping up a quick pan sauce.

• SAUTÉED CHICKEN, BEEF, PORK OR FISH WITH A PAN SAUCE •

PREP: 5 minutes   COOK: 8 – 15 minutes

INGREDIENTS
  2 boneless, skinless chicken breasts, pounded to about 1/2-inch thick, or
  1 (12 ounce) pork tenderloin, sliced into 6 medallions and pounded to 1/2-inch thick, or
  2 pork chops, or
  1 (12 ounce) ribeye, NY strip, or flat iron steak, or
  2 (6 ounce) salmon, grouper, cod, or mahi-mahi fillets
  Kosher salt and freshly ground pepper to taste
  1 tablespoon olive or canola oil
  1/4 cup beef or chicken broth
  1/4 cup white or red wine
  1 tablespoon unsalted butter

DIRECTIONS
  1.   Heat a 10-inch skillet over medium-high heat. Add the oil and swirl to coat. Add the chicken, meat, or fish and sauté until they reach the desired temperature (160° for the chicken, 145° for the pork, until the beef is to your liking, or the fish until if flakes easily with a fork. Anywhere from 8 – 12 minutes total).

  2.   Remove the chicken, pork, beef or fish to a plate and cover to keep warm. Reduce heat to medium and stir in the broth and wine. Scrap up any brown bits tin the bottom of the pan. Cook, stirring, until reduced by about half. Stir in butter to melt and poor the sauce over the chicken, pork, beef or fish.

ADDITIONAL OPTIONS
Stir any or all of these into the sauce before reducing:
  1 clove garlic
  1 teaspoon Dijon mustard
  3/4 cup canned chopped tomatoes
  1/2 teaspoon dried herbs of choice (or 1 teaspoon fresh)

• NO-COOK SAUCE FOR SAUTÉED •
CHICKEN, PORK, BEEF OR FISH

INGREDIENTS
   1/2 cup plain Greek yogurt

   1 tablespoons fresh lemon juice

   1/4 teaspoon minced or pressed garlic

   1/4 teaspoon salt

DIRECTIONS
   1.   Combine all of the ingredients in a small bowl and spoon over chicken, pork, beef or fish.

• AMPING UP BOTTLED BARBEQUE SAUCE •

Purchase an 18-ounce bottle of your preferred barbeque sauce (As mentioned earlier, I like Bull's-Eye or Sweet Baby Ray's).

- Add sautéed onions and garlic

- For smoky heat: finely chopped chipotle pepper (or put in a blender for a smoother sauce)

- For a bright tang: orange, pineapple, lime or lemon or a combination (2/3 cup for 18-oz bottle)

- For a fruity depth: Preserves like marmalade, apricot, peach, raspberry, blueberry (1/3 cup to start)

- For a touch of malt: thin with a light-bodied lager

- For a bit of complexity: red wine

- The ultimate: bourbon: 2 – 4 tablespoons or more to taste

• EASY-PEASY CHEESE SAUCE FOR VEGGIES, PASTA OR MEATS •

This will make 1-1/2 cups of sauce. Feel free to reduce the recipe by half if desired.

INGREDIENTS

3/4 cup half & half, divided

2 teaspoons cornstarch

8 ounces freshly grated cheese of choice (cheddar, Parmesan, Monterey jack, etc), about 2 cups

Kosher salt and freshly ground pepper to taste

DIRECTIONS

1.   In a small saucepan, bring 1/2 cup of the half & half to a simmer. Meanwhile, whisk the cornstarch and remaining half & half together in a cup or small bowl. Whisk the cornstarch mixture into the simmering half & half and cook, whisking constantly, until the sauce thickens, about 1 minute. Slowly stir in the cheese until smooth. Serve over veggies, pasta, poultry, meat or fish.

• DECADENT DESSERT SAUCE •

My favorite for pound cake, fresh berries, and vanilla ice cream.

INGREDIENTS

2 tablespoons sugar

1/2 cup water

1 tablespoons lemon juice

2 tablespoons Grand Marnier

1/2 lb (approx 1/2 pint) strawberries, hulled and halved

DIRECTIONS

1.   Combine sugar, water and lemon juice in a saucepan.

2.   Stir over medium heat until sugar is dissolved.

3.   Bring to a boil, reduce heat to low and simmer, uncovered, for about 5 minutes or until mixture becomes slightly syrupy.

4.   Remove from heat, stir in Grand Marnier and strawberries and spoon over cakes or ice cream.

CHAPTER 51

IF LAUGHTER IS THE BEST MEDICINE, I'LL NEVER GET SICK

I love to laugh.

But you may have already guessed that.

Slap a Charlie Chaplin or Buster Keaton movie in the DVD player, place a Tim Dorsey novel on my nightstand, let me binge-watch episodes of 30 Rock, or put me around the grill with the likes of Michael and Andy and you'll know what I mean. I feel healthier just thinking about it.

At this rate, I just might kick Methuselah's butt.

But it's just not the laughter that keeps me young.

No. It's meeting each day surrounded by family and friends who root for one another.

It's a wife that doesn't stand for any bull crap but still laughs at most of my jokes.

It's the friendships that outlast the three shots of single malt we all downed at Flanagan's Pub.

It's the readers whose eyes follow each vowel and consonant that I joyfully place on these pages.

It's the parties I attend where the guest of honor is someone whose name doesn't start with "Warren".

And it's the food. Always the food. Especially a hearty bowl of soup. (I've included a unique some twists on a few chowders below.)

I feel it every time I partake of a meal that someone has poured themselves into. It's what I want to offer every time I create a meal for others.

I live and exist because of what someone has taken the time to do for me. And I can only give thanks. Oh...And if you throw in a glass or two of wine, I'm sure we will laugh as well.

Good Food. Good Drink. All prepared for us by those who love us and nurture us.

Here are a few interesting chowders to make for your loved ones.

• SOUTHWESTERN CORN CHOWDER •

Corn chowders are popular back in Pennsylvania where my wife is from. I even included an excellent recipe in my book Table for Two. But since we're cooking outside the lines, I thought I'd add this spicy rendition to the repertoire.

PREP: 10 minutes   COOK: 40 minutes

INGREDIENTS
- 1 tablespoon olive oil
- 1 medium onion, finely chopped (about 1 cup)
- 2 cloves garlic, minced
- 1 small jalapeno pepper, seeded and minced
- 1/4 teaspoon kosher salt
- 2 teaspoons cumin
- 3 cups chicken or vegetable broth
- 1 medium sweet potato, peeled and diced (about 2 cups)
- 1/2 red bell pepper, chopped
- 3 cups corn kernels
- Lime wedges and chopped fresh cilantro to garnish

DIRECTIONS
1. Heat olive oil in a medium dutch oven over medium-high heat. Add onions and sauté until soft and translucent, about 8 minutes. Add garlic, jalapeño pepper, salt and cumin and sauté for 2 more minutes.

2. Add broth and potatoes and bring to a boil. Turn heat to low and simmer, covered until potatoes are tender, about 10 minutes.

3. Add red pepper and corn and simmer for 10 more minutes.

4. Puree half the soup in a blender or food processor. Return to the pot and reheat.

Sprinkle cilantro on top of each bowl and serve with lime wedges.

• SALMON CHOWDER •

When most of us think of a seafood-based chowder, we immediately think of clam chowder. I have a pretty good recipe in my other cookbook. But here's a nice change that's inspired by my friends in the Pacific Northwest.

PREP:10 minutes   COOK: 20 minutes

INGREDIENTS

1 pound boneless, skinless salmon fillets, cut into 1-inch pieces

3 tablespoons unsalted butter

1/2 medium red bell pepper, chopped

3 medium red potatoes, cut into 1/2-inch dice

1 cup chicken broth or clam juice (or a combination of the two)

1-1/2 cups milk

1/2 cup heavy cream

1/2 teaspoon kosher salt

Pinch of cayenne pepper

Chopped fresh parsley, green scallion tops, or chives to garnish.

DIRECTIONS

1. Heat a large saucepan over medium-high heat. Add the butter to melt. Stir in the onions and bell pepper and sauté until soft, about 6 – 8 minutes.

2. Stir in the potatoes and broth. Reduce heat to medium and simmer until the potatoes are softened, about 6 – 8 minutes.

3. Stir in the salmon, milk, cream, salt and cayenne pepper. Simmer until the salmon flakes easily with a fork, about 5 minutes. Ladle into bowls and garnish with the parsley.

• POOR MAN'S LOBSTER AND CORN CHOWDER •

For those of you who've had the opportunity to attend one of my shows, you know that I'm a frugal chef. So it won't surprise you to find that I've included a lobster chowder recipe that contains no lobster. Don't get me wrong. I love lobster. But it ain't cheap. Especially if you just buy the frozen meat. This recipe calls for 2 cups, which is about a pound of lobster meat. So in keeping with my frugal nature, we're going to make this with "poor man's lobster" which is monkfish. It's a fraction of the price of lobster, yet comes close to mirroring the texture and flavor.

PREP: 10 minutes   COOK: 35 minutes

INGREDIENTS
   1 pound monkfish cut into 1 inch pieces
   3 tablespoons unsalted butter
   1 medium onion, chopped (about 1 cup)
   1 red bell pepper, chopped
   1/2 teaspoon thyme
   1/4 teaspoon marjoram
   1/2 teaspoon kosher salt
   1/2 teaspoon freshly ground pepper
   1/2 teaspoon sugar
   3 medium red potatoes, cut into 1/2-inch dice
   3 cups milk
   2-1/2 cups frozen corn

DIRECTIONS
1.   Heat a large saucepan over medium-high heat. Add the butter and swirl to coat. Add the onion and red pepper and sauté until soft, about 8 minutes.

2.   Stir in the thyme, marjoram, salt, pepper, sugar and potatoes. Cook for 1 minute. Stir in the milk and bring to a boil. Reduce heat to medium-low and simmer until the potatoes have softened, about 15 minutes.

3.   Stir in the corn and monkfish and simmer until the monkfish is firm, about 10 minutes longer.

• VEGETABLE CHOWDER •

Don't let the name fool you. This recipe will start a party in your mouth. It seems like a lot of ingredients, but it's mostly veggies. Feel free to tweak it according to the veggies you have on hand.

PREP:10 minutes   COOK: 30 minutes

INGREDIENTS

2 tablespoons unsalted butter or olive oil

1 medium onion, chopped (about 1 cup)

1 celery ribs, diced

1 carrot peeled a diced, about 1/2 cup

1 medium red potato, diced

1-1/2 cups vegetable broth or water

1/4 teaspoon thyme

1 small bay leaf

1 teaspoons kosher salt

1/4 teaspoon freshly ground black pepper

1/4 cup frozen cut green beans

1/4 cup diced red bell pepper (you can use jarred)

1/2 cup diced zucchini or yellow squash

1/4 cup frozen peas

1 tablespoons chopped fresh parsley

1 cups milk

1/2 cup grated cheddar cheese, grated

1 ounce cream cheese

DIRECTIONS

1. Heat a large saucepan over medium heat. Add the butter or oil and swirl to coat. Add the onions and sauté until soft, about 8 minutes. Stir in the celery, cover, and cook until the celery softens, stirring occasionally. About 3 - 5 minutes.

2. Add the carrots, potatoes, broth, thyme, bay leaf, salt, and pepper and bring to a boil. Reduce heat, cover, and simmer until the vegetables are just tender, about 5 minutes.

3. With a strainer or slotted spoon, remove about 3/4 cup of the cooked vegetables and place in a blender.

4. Add the green beans, bell peppers, and zucchini to the saucepan and cook until the green beans are tender, about 5 minutes. Stir in the peas and parsley, simmer for 2 more minutes, and then remove from the heat. Discard the bay leaf.

5. Meanwhile, puree the reserved vegetables with the milk and cheeses to make a smooth sauce.

Stir the sauce into the soup and gently reheat.

CHAPTER 52

REFRIGERATOR SOUP – HOW TO FEED YOUR FAMILY AND GUESTS WITH LEFTOVERS FROM THE FRIDGE

In the last chapter I shared some killer chowders. But there are some nights when I ditch formal recipes and whip up a batch of "Refrigerator Soup". Although this soup is known by other names: "Clean Out the Freezer Soup", "Dump Soup" (as in clean out the fridge and dump it all into a pot), "Kitchen Sink Soup" or my favorite, especially when I'm preparing this for company: "Soupe du les Restes Nourriture", you'll not find an easier soup to make on this planet.

I learned to make Refrigerator Soup out of necessity, not because I wanted to be clever. When my kids were younger and still living at home we had a rule in our kitchen: if you finish it, you wash it. Did you drink the last glass of iced tea? Then wash the pitcher. Did you finish that leftover pasta? Then wash the bowl. Did you eat that last piece of chicken or steak? Then wash the plate. Did you finish up those veggies? Then wash the Tupperware container.

You get my drift.

Trouble was, at the end of the week our fridge would be filled with dishes, bowls and plastic containers that had just a few bites of chicken or meat, a forkful or two of pasta, a couple of teaspoons of veggies, one dollop of mashed potatoes, a meager quarter-cup of rice, etc.

Confronted with this plethora of culinary detritus in dozens of containers, my kids would say, "But dad, I didn't finish it!"

Sigh… I couldn't get too upset by their strategy. I did the same thing when I was a kid.

So instead of tossing out all of these leftovers, I'd whip up some refrigerator soup. It was always delicious. And it was always different. I've even served it to company.

I'm sure if you're reading this book, you have leftovers in the fridge, too. So let's pull out whatever's there and get cooking.

I know that after making this soup a few times, you'll find yourself making a little more food than required for a particular meal just so you can have some leftovers for Refrigerator Soup.

I do.

• BASIC REFRIGERATOR SOUP •

INGREDIENTS

4 cups beef, chicken or veggie broth

2 cups (or more) cooked leftovers

Kosher salt and freshly ground pepper to taste

DIRECTIONS

In a medium saucepan, bring broth and leftovers to a boil over medium-high heat. Reduce heat to a simmer until everything is heated though. Serve with a salad and warm bread for a complete meal.

VARIATIONS

If you have the time, dice a medium onion and sauté in a little olive or vegetable oil in the saucepan until soft, about 5 minutes. Add one clove of garlic and sauté for one additional minute. Add the broth and leftovers and continue as above.

Stir in a half (or full) can of diced tomatoes, with or without juice.

Stir in a half (or full) can of beans, rinsed and drained.

Stir in a half-teaspoon herb of choice (I like thyme).

Sprinkle each bowl with grated Parmesan cheese.

Stir in one tablespoon sherry to each bowl before serving.

Place broth and leftovers in a blender and puree before cooking.

These are just a few ideas I've tried...I'm sure between the two of us we can come up with a few more!

CHAPTER 53

I GOT KICKED OUT OF THE LIBRARY, BUT I GOT MY REVENGE AND STILL HAD TIME TO MAKE A GREAT MEAL

I got booted from the library this week. Tuesday to be exact.

I was relaxing in a chair in the magazine section flipping through back issues of *The Enlightened Sous Chef* when someone called me on my cell phone. I answered and tried to talk in whispers so as not to disturb anyone who was actually there to read. Then this librarian scurried over and tapped me on the shoulder.

"Excuse me, sir, but didn't you see the sign? You're not allowed to use a cell phone in the library."

I glanced up at her. "But I'm not using a cell phone".

"Oh?" she said, raising one eyebrow. "Then what's that thing you're holding up to your ear?"

"It's a pacemaker. For my brain. See, whenever I forget something or loose my train of thought, this little baby jumpstarts my thought process."

She placed her hands on her hips and leaned forward. "Then how come I saw you talking into it?"

"It's voice activated," I replied with a smile. "It only comes on when I speak. I save a fortune on batteries."

She didn't buy it, and I found myself out on the street.

So I got back at them.

The next day I went back and checked out, like, 27 books. But instead of leaving with them, I put them all back on the shelf.

Ha! Let 'em figure that one out.

And while they're scratching their heads over that one, let me share some ham steak recipes I managed to scribble down on the back of my library card. They're from *The Enlightened Sous Chef Issue #86 – The Swimsuit Edition.*

• HAM STEAK WITH MAPLE-MUSTARD GLAZE •

PREP: 5 minutes   COOK: 10 minutes

INGREDIENTS

   1/2 center-cut ready-to-eat ham steak, about 3/4 pound

   3 tablespoons maple syrup

   2 teaspoons apple cider vinegar

   2 teaspoons Dijon mustard.

DIRECTIONS

1. Preheat the broiler.

2. Line a shallow rimmed baking pan with foil and place a rack in the pan. Place
    the ham steak on the rack in the baking pan or the rack of a broiler pan.

3. In a small bowl, combine the maple syrup, cider vinegar and mustard until
    smooth. Brush the glaze mixture over the ham steak.

4. Broil the ham about 3 to 4 inches from the heat source until the glaze is
    bubbling and lightly browned, about 4 minutes. Turn the ham over and
    baste with more of the maple mustard mixture; broil for another 3 to 5
    minutes, until browned.

• FRUIT GLAZED HAM STEAKS •

I love this because I can change it up by switching out the fruit preserves. And please, you must use fruit preserves (like Smuckers®) not fruit jelly!

PREP: 5 minutes   COOK: 10 minutes

INGREDIENTS
  1/2 center-cut ready-to-eat ham steak, about 3/4 pound
  1-1/2 tablespoons brown sugar
  2 tablespoons apricot, peach, blueberry, strawberry preserves or marmalade
  2 teaspoons Dijon mustard

DIRECTIONS
  1.   Preheat the broiler.

  2.   Line a shallow rimmed baking pan with foil and place a rack in the pan. Place the ham steak on the rack in the baking pan or the rack of a broiler pan.

  3.   In a small bowl, combine the brown sugar, preserves and mustard until smooth. Brush the glaze mixture over the ham steak.

  4.   Broil the ham about 3 to 4 inches from the heat source until the glaze is bubbling and lightly browned, about 4 minutes. Turn the ham over and baste with more of the maple mustard mixture; broil for another 3 to 5 minutes, until browned.

CHAPTER 54

BAGPIPES, BANGOS, AND FRIED CALAMARI

There's nothing like volunteering at the local "Y" to give one a sense of civic pride. I once helped coach a basketball team of 7 – 9 year olds. Fortunately, my co-coach knew all about the game of basketball and had actually played it a few times. As for me? Well, I guess he brought me in to raise the team's collective self-esteem, because each one of those little guys could kick my butt in a game of one-on-one. But I had one thing they didn't have – a whistle.

And here's what I found out. A whistle is a lot like the bagpipes, only easier to play. I always wanted my parents to buy me a set of bagpipes for my 16th birthday (to honor my Scots/Irish heritage). It didn't happen. They told me there was no place to practice them without disturbing the neighbors. I told them I could always drive down the interstate and hold them out the window.

They nixed that idea as well. They figured by the time I was 18 I'd have been pulled over at least a dozen times for practicing.

Thankfully, my love for the bagpipes prepared me for my job with the Nature Conservancy. At the interview they asked me if I loved working with sea creatures. I told them, yeah. They asked how much. I said, a lot. They asked if I'd ever wrangled an octopus. I said, no, but I always wanted to play the bagpipes. They said that was close enough, and I got the job. Being around all that ocean is when I learned to cook calamari.

But the bagpipes wouldn't have been my first instrument. That would've been the trumpet. Everyone in the 5th grade at Daniel Warren Elementary in the 60's had to learn an instrument. My first choice? The violin. Probably because Larry from The Three Stooges wreaked so much havoc with his. (Remember when his bow took that guy's toupee off in the courtroom? I so wanted to do that.)

Anyway, it seemed that most of my classmates had the exact same idea. The school ran out of violins, so they gave me a trumpet.

And here's what I learned: One should never take a trumpet to the beach to practice. Do you know how much sand a 5th grader can cram into the horn of a trumpet? Trust me. A lot. Especially if he takes off his sneaker and uses it to really cram it in.

The next day I turned my trumpet back in to the music teacher because the plungers kept sticking and the mouthpiece tasted like salt. After muttering some words that sounded a lot like "you little muffin shucker", he snatched the trumpet out of my hand and issued me a triangle in its place.

But that was okay. Now I could at least practice at the beach.

Later on, in college, I picked up the banjo. Got pretty good at it, too. In the late 70's, I was voted 2nd best banjo player in the state of Florida. I'd show you my trophy but the engraver misspelled the word 'banjo'. He spelled it 'bango' (like I was playing a tropical fruit as it might be pronounced by someone with a sinus infection).

I hope you've been able to follow my random thoughts on bagpipes, bangos, octopi and calamari.

And although calamari might resemble a small octopus, it's really quite different. Here's a classic recipe that I'm sure you will enjoy. Scaled down for two, of course. And since we are cooking outside the lines, I've included a recipe for aioli for the dipping sauce. It's a nice change from the usual marinara sauce.

• SIMPLE AIOLI •

INGREDIENTS
   6 tablespoons mayonnaise
   2 cloves garlic, minced or pressed
   4 teaspoons fresh lemon juice
   1/4 teaspoon kosher salt

Combine all ingredients in a small bowl and mix well. Refrigerate for 15 – 30 minutes.

• FRIED CALAMARI •

It hasn't always been easy to find calamari (squid) in your neighborhood grocery store. Now, thankfully, many carry it cleaned and ready to cook at the seafood counter or in the frozen food section. If your grocery store doesn't carry it, your local fish market most certainly will. This recipe is a northern Italian classic which is why I also included an aioli dipping sauce (Calamari with tomato sauce is an American invention). Follow this up with a Caesar Salad and you'll have a nice weeknight meal.

PREP: 15 minutes
COOK: 5 minutes

SOAK: 15 minutes

INGREDIENTS

1/2 pound calamari, cleaned

3/4 cup milk

1 egg

3 fresh basil leaves, chopped

Enough canola or vegetable oil to fill skillet to 1-inch

1 cup all-purpose flour

1 teaspoon paprika

1/2 teaspoon cayenne pepper

1/2 teaspoon dried oregano

1/2 teaspoon kosher salt

1/4 teaspoon ground black pepper

Lemon wedges to garnish

DIRECTIONS

1. Rinse the calamari and pat dry. Cut the body into 1/2-inch rings and trim the tentacles as desired.

2. Combine the milk, egg, and basil leaves in a small bowl. Beat until well mixed. Place the calamari into the mixture and refrigerate for 15 minutes. Prepare Aioli Sauce (below) and refrigerate.

3. Meanwhile, combine the flour, paprika, cayenne pepper, oregano, salt and pepper in a bowl.

4. Heat the oil in a cast iron skillet or heavy pot over medium heat until the temperature reaches 375°.

5. Dredge the calamari in the seasoned flour to coat, then fry for 1 to 3 minutes until golden brown. Remove with a slotted spoon and drain on paper towels. Serve immediately with lemon wedges or an aioli dipping sauce.

• CAESAR SALAD •

Sure, you can make this with store-bought garlic croutons, but why not whip up some of your own? It's a great way to use up day-old bread.

INGREDIENTS

2 cloves garlic, peeled, 1 clove crushed, one clove quartered

1/4 cup mayonnaise

3 anchovy fillets, minced (or 2 teaspoons anchovy paste)

3 tablespoons grated Parmesan cheese, divided

1/2 teaspoon Worcestershire sauce

1/2 teaspoon Dijon mustard

1/2 tablespoon lemon juice

Kosher salt and freshly ground black pepper to taste

1-1/2 tablespoons extra virgin olive oil

1 cup day-old bread, cubed

1/2 head romaine lettuce (or two hearts of romaine) torn into bite-size pieces

DIRECTIONS

1. In a small bowl whisk together the crushed garlic, mayonnaise, anchovies, 1 tablespoon of the Parmesan cheese, Worcestershire sauce, mustard, and lemon juice. Season to taste with salt and black pepper.

2. Heat the oil in a 10-inch skillet over medium heat. Add the garlic quarters and sauté until the garlic is golden and fragrant, about 2 - 3 minutes. Remove garlic from pan and add bread cubes. Cook, turning frequently, until lightly browned. Remove bread cubes and season with salt and pepper.

3. Place lettuce pieces in a medium bowl. Add the dressing, remaining Parmesan cheese, and seasoned bread cubes then toss.

CHAPTER 55

SOMETIMES DINING OUT IS A LOT LIKE HAVING YOUR FACE SUCKED THROUGH A COLANDER. ONLY MORE SO

I rarely go out to eat anymore. It's just too painful.

It's not that I harbor an aversion to letting someone else do all the cooking, serving, and cleaning up. It's just that, well, so many restaurants seem to do it so badly these days. Especially the serving part.

I know there are still establishments scattered around the country where it's almost impossible to get a job waiting tables unless you were fortunate enough to have inherited the position from a parent or relative. I'm thinking of the likes of the former Charlie Trotter's in Chicago, or Le Bernardin in Manhattan, or even Bern's Steakhouse in Tampa. Landing a server position at one of those venerable institutions would be akin to winning the lottery.

No. I'm talking about the other 95% of the restaurants that dot our highways and byways. The ones where the red-headed and barely post-teen hostess greets everyone with a smile as sweet and natural as a packet of Splenda and gushes, "So how are you guys tonight?" Even if the party is made up of a half-dozen septuagenarian women fresh from a late-afternoon game of bridge.

You know the type and I know the type. It's the effervescent gum-popping blonde whose cell phone is surgically affixed to her ear. Or the middle-aged woman who is convinced she can take the orders from three different tables simultaneously and effectively. Or the gangly 20-something waiter with the dreadlocked ponytail and an order pad stuffed down the front of his pants.

I can sense some of you nodding in agreement.

However, I've been known to overlook my server's hairstyle, order-taking strategies, or technological accouterments if the food and service are exceptional. Heck, I own a cell phone, and I once sported a ponytail. But there are occasions when it's hard to ignore certain examples of dining room buffoonery.

Like the time my fiancée, now wife, ordered warm apple pie à la mode. The waitress presented her with a pie that was as nearly as cold as the vanilla ice cream that crowned it. When I pointed this out to the waitress, she snatched it up and replied, "I'm sorry. I'll be right back."

You're probably guessing what happened next.

The waitress returned a few minutes later with the same plate of pie and ice cream, but after she had obviously nuked it for a minute or two in the microwave. True, the apple pie was now as warm as a baby's cuddle, but the ice cream had completely melted over the pie, creating a thick, dull white pool that oozed across the plate. Yum.

Or the time I ordered a chef's salad with Dijon vinaigrette on the side. When the waitress placed my salad in front of me, I kindly asked if she would bring my side of salad dressing. She said she had already added it. I stared at my naked salad as she continued, "I poured it down the side of the bowl just like you asked me to. It's probably all at the bottom."

Or the time I ordered a medium-rare rib eye and received one that was plainly well-done. When I pointed this out to the waiter, he offered to take it back to the kitchen so the chef could fix it. (Short of firing up the time machine they must've had stashed back there, I'm not sure what the chef could've done to "fix" my steak).

Or the time my date ordered her eggs once-over-light and was presented with an order that was unmistakably scrambled. When I reminded the waitress that my companion had requested eggs over light, the waitress replied that she had, indeed, seen the cook turn them over once, but she would go back and check with him just to be sure.

Hmm. Now that I think of it. Being greeted at the door by a bouncy redhead with a "How're you guys, tonight?" doesn't sound so bad after all. Even if your 79-year-old mother is with you.

Now, hand me that colander, will ya?

No wait; let's not dine out. Maybe we should just whip up a gourmet restaurant meal here at home.

I'm thinking Poisson en Papillote (fish baked in paper - but to simply things we'll use aluminum foil in lieu of the paper). It won't take long and it's absolutely delish.

You with me?

• BASIC FISH IN A PACKET •

Once you make this easy, foolproof dish, I guarantee you'll make it often!

PREP: 5 minutes   COOK: 20 minutes

INGREDIENTS
    2 sheets aluminum foil, 12 x 24 inches
    2 (4 - 6 ounce) tilapia fillets, rinsed and patted dry
    1/2 sweet onion, sliced
    1/2 tablespoon olive oil, divided
    1 teaspoon unsalted butter, melted
    1 teaspoon lemon pepper (or other favorite fish seasoning)
    4 lemon slices (optional)

DIRECTIONS
1.   Preheat oven to 450°.

2.   Fold each sheet of foil in half to make a 12-inch square. Brush the center of each square with olive oil. Place sliced onion rings on aluminum foil, place filets on top, drizzle with oil and butter and sprinkle on seasoning, top with lemon slices (if using).

3.   Fold the foil into air-tight packets and bake for 20 minutes. Carefully open one packet to ensure that the fish is opaque and flakes easily.

Transfer packet contents to a plate or bowl to serve.

Serve with Green Beans and Steamed White Rice.

• MEDITERRANEAN FISH IN A PACKET •

While this is almost a meal in itself, I like to serve this with a simple salad.

PREP:10 minutes   COOK: 20 minutes

INGREDIENTS

2 sheets aluminum foil, 12 x 24 inches

Extra virgin olive oil, as needed

2 (4 - 6 ounce) tilapia fillets, rinsed and patted dry

2 tablespoons olive oil

2 teaspoons fresh lemon juice

Kosher salt and freshly ground pepper to taste

4 cloves of garlic, roughly chopped

1 red or sweet yellow onions, diced

2 cups baby spinach leaves

4 plum tomatoes, roughly chopped (you can used canned tomatoes)

2 tablespoons balsamic vinegar

1 tablespoons chopped fresh basil, or 1 teaspoon dried

1 tablespoons chopped fresh parsley

Red pepper flakes, to taste

DIRECTIONS

1. Preheat oven to 450°.

2. Fold each sheet of foil in half to make a 12-inch square. Brush the center of each square with olive oil. Lay the fish fillets in the center. Squeeze a little lemon juice over the fillets. Season with salt and pepper to taste.

3. In a medium bowl, combine the garlic, onion, baby spinach and tomatoes. Add the balsamic vinegar, herbs, red pepper flakes and toss to mix. Drizzle with enough extra virgin olive oil to moisten it all. Toss to coat.

4. Spoon the spinach-tomato mixture on top of the fish. Drizzle on any remaining olive oil left in the bowl.

5. Fold the foil into air-tight packets and bake for 20 minutes. Carefully open one packet to ensure that the fish is opaque and flakes easily.

Serve over Steamed White Rice.

• CARIBBEAN FISH IN A PACKET •

You can make this refreshing seafood entrée a little hotter if you keep the seeds and ribs in the jalapeno peppers.

PREP:10 minutes   COOK: 20 minutes

INGREDIENTS

2 sheets aluminum foil, 12 x 24 inches

Extra virgin olive oil, as needed

2 (4 - 6 ounce) tilapia fillets, rinsed and patted dry

2 tablespoons olive oil

1 small tomato, thinly sliced

3 scallions, chopped (with some of the green)

2 tablespoons fresh cilantro

2 tablespoons fresh lime juice

1/2 jalapeño pepper, minced (seeds and membrane removed for a milder taste) or a few drops of hot sauce

Kosher salt and freshly ground pepper to taste

DIRECTIONS

1. Preheat oven to 450°.

2. Fold each sheet of foil in half to make a 12-inch square. Brush the center of each square with olive oil. Lay the fish fillets in the center. Top each fillet with half the tomatoes, the sprinkle with olive oil, scallions, cilantro, lime juice, pepper or hot pepper sauce, salt and black pepper.

3. Fold the foil into air-tight packets and bake for 20 minutes. Carefully open one packet to ensure that the fish is opaque and flakes easily.

Serve over Steamed White Rice.

• ASIAN FISH IN A PACKET •

You can make this recipe without the chili oil but I recommend that you don't. The amount of oil will not make this dish hot, but it will give it a subtle depth.

PREP:10 minutes   COOK: 20 minutes

INGREDIENTS
  2 sheets aluminum foil, 12 x 24 inches
  2 (4 - 6 ounce) tilapia fillets, rinsed and patted dry
  2 tablespoons olive oil, divided
  1 cup cooked rice
  2 cups coarsely chopped bok choy (or other greens like kale)
  2 scallions, chopped (with some of the green)
  1 teaspoon fresh grated ginger
  1 clove garlic, minced or pressed
  2 tablespoons soy sauce
  2 teaspoons dark sesame oil
  2 dashes chili oil (optional)

DIRECTIONS
  1.   Preheat oven to 450°.

  2.   Fold each sheet of foil in half to make a 12-inch square. Brush the center of each square with olive oil. Spread half the rice on the center of each sheet of foil, then layer the greens, fish and scallions on top of the rice.

  3.   In a small bowl, combine 1 tablespoon olive oil, grated ginger, garlic, soy sauce, sesame oil and chili oil (if using).

  4.   Pour the sauce over each serving. Fold the foil into air-tight packets and bake for 20 minutes. Carefully open one packet to ensure that the fish is opaque and flakes easily.

Serve over Steamed White Rice.

• FLORIDIAN FISH IN A PACKET •

Because I live in Florida, I had to include this tropical version. Don't worry; you won't need any exotic ingredients. Just pour a glass of fruity wine and you'll feel like you're dining oceanside.

PREP: 10 minutes   COOK: 10 minutes

INGREDIENTS
   2 sheets aluminum foil, 12 x 24 inches
   2 (4 - 6 ounce) tilapia fillets, rinsed and patted dry
   Kosher salt and freshly ground pepper to taste
   1 (4 x 1/2-inch) strip orange peel, cut into thin slivers
   1/2 tablespoon slivered fresh basil
   3/4 cup chopped tomatoes
   2 tablespoons finely chopped red onion
   2 teaspoons orange juice
   1 Tbsp olive oil

DIRECTIONS
   1.   Preheat oven to 450°.

   2.   Fold each sheet of foil in half to make a 12-inch square. Brush the center of each square with olive oil. Place 1 fish fillet in center of each square. Sprinkle with salt and pepper; top with orange peel and basil.

   3.   In a small bowl, combine the tomatoes, onions orange juice and olive oil. Spoon over fish.

   3.   Spoon half the olive oil mixture over each fillet. Fold the foil into air-tight packets and bake for 20 minutes. Carefully open one packet to ensure that the fish is opaque and flakes easily.

Serve over Steamed White Rice.

• FRENCH FISH IN A PACKET •

And this is where it all began, Poisson en Papillote. Enjoy this classic dish with candlelight and a nice white wine.

PREP: 10 minutes   COOK: 20 minutes

INGREDIENTS
    2 sheets aluminum foil, 12 x 24 inches
    2 (4 - 6 ounce) tilapia fillets, rinsed and patted dry
    1 small zucchini or yellow squash, thinly sliced
    1 cup sliced mushrooms (I like baby portobellos)
    1/2 medium red or sweet onion, thinly sliced
    2 tablespoons olive oil
    3 tablespoons fresh lemon juice
    1/4 cup dry white wine
    1 tablespoon chopped fresh marjoram or basil (or 1 teaspoon dried)
    6 black kalamata olives, pitted and halved

DIRECTIONS
1. Preheat oven to 450°.

2. Fold each sheet of foil in half to make a 12-inch square. Brush the center of each square with olive oil. Place half the zucchini, mushrooms, fish and onions in the center of each sheet of foil in that order.

3. In a small bowl, combine the olive oil, lemon juice, white wine, and marjoram or basil.

4. Spoon half the olive oil mixture over each fillet and top with black olives. Fold the foil into air-tight packets and bake for 20 minutes. Carefully open one packet to ensure that the fish is opaque and flakes easily.

Serve over Steamed White Rice.

CHAPTER 56

WHY I DON'T EAT ON PLANES. OR ANYWHERE NEAR AN AIRPORT

Is it just me, or has flying gotten crazier these days? Back in October I flew from Orlando, Florida to Lexington, Kentucky.

Since it was on the way, we made a three-hour stop in Detroit. (Which, of course, makes complete sense if the booking agent doesn't own a map.)

After counting the layover and early arrival time to participate in the TSA security procedures, it took me almost nine hours to fly to a city I could've driven to in eleven.

And the price for this convenience? Around $300.

I was smarter when I had to fly to Kentucky a second time in December. This time I chose Allegiant Air. They offer nonstop flights from Orlando to Kentucky and they're dirt cheap.

Round-trip cost? $79. Of course, if you want food, drinks, or choice of seat, you have to pay extra.

Anyway, since I saved so much on airfare, I decided to forgo the Standard TSA Body Search and upgraded to the Enhanced Pat-Down Option. I even slipped the woman assigned to me an extra $10 so that she would warm her hands first.

That was the best $10 I ever spent.

Unfortunately, when I had to fly to the Detroit area for an appearance at the International Women's Show, I not only skimped on the $10 hand-warming fee, I even took advantage of the $25 discount they give if you opt for Basic Groping in lieu of the Standard Body Search. I was rewarded with a visit from a guy whose name tag read Boris. He was a double hand amputee and sported stainless steel claws at the ends of his arms.

That was the worst $25 I ever saved. (Note to self: Obviously the words, "Please be gentle" when translated into Ukrainian means, "Is that all you got, ugly man?")

After applying a few strategically placed bandages and donning a new pair of underwear, I joined the other passengers and flew to Detroit so that we could all deplane and wait 3 hours for our bags to arrive. It seems they were mis-routed to Dubuque (a common error since both cities begin with the letter 'D'). It was around dinner time and I was hungry. At first I thought about calling up a friend to meet me at a restaurant downtown, but all of the taxis at the airport had been hijacked by masked thugs with who needed rides to the next pillaging. After all, it was Detroit.

So I resigned myself to grab a bite at the airport. After all, airports have restaurants with familiar names like Sbarro's, Ruby Tuesday, Fuddruckers, and T.G.I. Friday's.

So I wandered from one restaurant to the other checking out their menus. I recognized the pictures, but I sure didn't recognize the prices. I hate paying the going rate for casual restaurant food as it is, but when they jack up the prices like these guys did? Fah-ged-aboud-it.

Yep, I sure learned my lesson. So on my next trip, I successfully smuggled in some roasted pork tenderloin, garlic smashed potatoes and steamed green beans in the lining of that ten-gallon hat I bought in Texas last year.

Boris the stainless steel TSA groper may be good, but he's not that good.

Say, would you like a glass of Chardonnay with your dish? I've got a bottle in my socks.

• GLAZED ROAST PORK TENDERLOIN – FOUR WAYS •

PREP: 10 minutes   COOK: 45 minutes

INGREDIENTS

3/4-pound pork tenderloin

1/4 teaspoon thyme

Kosher salt and freshly ground pepper to taste

1-1/2 tablespoons olive oil or canola oil

GLAZES

Apricot Glaze

1 clove garlic, crushed

1/2 cup apricot preserves

1/4 cup orange juice

1-1/2 teaspoons lemon juice

1 tablespoon honey

Honey Soy Glaze

3 tablespoons honey

1 tablespoon soy sauce

1-1/2 teaspoons brown sugar

1 tablespoon sesame oil

1 tablespoon balsamic vinegar

Brown Sugar and Mustard Glaze

1-1/2 tablespoons brown sugar

1 tablespoon grainy deli mustard

1 teaspoon rosemary

1 tablespoon dry sherry

Maple Syrup and Mustard Glaze

1 teaspoon sage

3 tablespoons real maple syrup

3 tablespoons apple cider vinegar

1 teaspoon Dijon mustard

DIRECTIONS

1. Preheat oven to 450°.

2. Pat tenderloin dry and season with thyme, salt and pepper. Heat olive oil in a 10-inch skillet over medium-high heat until it just begins to smoke. Add tenderloin and cook until brown on all sides, about 8 -10 minutes total. Transfer to a lightly oiled baking dish.

3. Add glaze ingredients to the pan and stir to dissolve the brown bits, about 3 minutes. Brush glaze over the tenderloin and roast, turning the tenderloin over once until an instant-read thermometer reads 135°, about 10 - 15 minutes.

4. Remove tenderloin to a cutting board and cover loosely with foil. Let rest until an instant-read thermometer registers 145°, about 5 - 10 minutes. Carve into 1/4 -inch slices and serve with Garlic Smashed Potatoes and Steamed Green Beans.

• GARLIC SMASHED POTATOES •

PREP: 5 minutes   COOK: 30 minutes

INGREDIENTS
  3/4 pound red potatoes, quartered
  2 tablespoons unsalted butter
  1 tablespoon chopped garlic
  1/4 cup milk, warmed
  1 tablespoon grated Parmesan cheese
  1/2 teaspoon kosher salt or to taste
  Pinch of white pepper

DIRECTIONS
1. Bring a large pot of salted water to a boil over medium high heat. Add potatoes and cook until tender but still firm, about 30 minutes; drain.

2. In the meantime, melt butter in an omelet pan and add garlic. Sauté for 1 - 2 minutes.

3. Stir in butter and garlic, milk, cheese, salt and pepper into potatoes and mash with a potato masher or large fork.

• STEAMED GREEN BEANS •

Place 1/2 pound green beans in a steamer basket over an inch or two of boiling water. Cover and steam for 8-12 minutes for whole beans until crisp-tender. Season with butter, kosher salt and freshly ground pepper to taste.

CHAPTER 57

TEN HOLIDAY KITCHEN SAFETY TIPS YOU DON'T WANT TO MISS

If you don't count the hall bathroom after your wife's unemployed brother has spent the good part of the morning in it, the kitchen is the most dangerous and hazardous place in your home.

This is especially true during the holidays when an overwhelming majority of Americans assume they can actually cook.

So in the spirit of the season, I offer these 10 important holiday kitchen safety tips:

1.   Wash up as you work and keep your cooking area clean and clear. Keep potholders, towels, wooden utensils, food packaging, and curtains away from the stovetop. Oh, and remember that holiday tie you got from the kids? The one with Mickey Mouse dressed as Santa? Don't wear it if you're going to be hanging over the stove.

2.   Don't hold a child in your arms when you're working in the kitchen. Even if it's someone else's kid. The same goes for pets.

3.   There's usually a good reason the smoke alarm goes off. The good folks at First Alert did not create these items just to annoy the heck out of you.

4.   If you do have a grease fire in a pan or pot, quickly slide a lid over it to completely cut off the oxygen supply, then turn off the heat. Avoid the urge to immediately lift up the lid "just to take a peek."

5.   If the fire is in your oven, close the door and turn off the heat to smother the flames. Don't worry about the turkey in there. It's probably a goner.

6.   If the fire is in your microwave oven, turn it off immediately and keep the door closed until the fire is completely out. Unplug the appliance if you can safely reach the outlet.

7.   If the fire is in your belly, it's probably a good sign. You really do need to get off that lazy butt of yours and do something with your life.

8.   Best option for fires? Purchase a multipurpose dry-chemical extinguisher rated for Class A, B and C fires. Hang it in an easily accessible place in your kitchen, not in the garage. And remember, this device is not a toy. Sticking the hose down the back of Uncle Roy's shorts and giving him "one good shot for old time's sake" might seem funny to you and almost everybody else in the room, but it'll probably piss Uncle Roy off real bad.

9. Nuke your dirty sponges occasionally in the microwave for one minute to kill any bacteria that might be present. Important Note: Make sure the sponge is damp when you do this, or it may catch on fire (see Important Kitchen Safety Tip # 6).

10. And finally, avoid cross-contamination. Don't toss a salad with the fork that you used to scramble eggs. And don't use the same cutting board to cut raw veggies and raw meat.

Bonus Tips:
1. Put on an apron. You want to share your culinary creation, not wear it.

2. However, donning an apron does not give you permission to wear that striped shirt with the plaid pants you bought for the golf outing. The focus should be on the food. Not you.

3. Resist the urge to also wear that 3-foot tall chef's toque you bought at Williams-Sonoma for just this occasion. You'll only get it stuck in the exhaust fan over the stove. Ditto for the big elf's hat you got from the secret Santa at this year's office party.

4. If you want to be funny, don't recite the pledge of allegiance when you volunteer to say 'grace'. Everyone at the table has seen *Christmas Vacation*. It was funnier in the movie.

CHAPTER 58

TOFURKEY: WHO INVENTED THIS, AND WHY DO THEY HATE US SO?

According to a leading online encyclopedia the word tofurkey is a portmanteau word of tofu and turkey (For those of you who don't know, *portmanteau* is the French word for the blending of two silly sounding words into one even sillier sounding word.)

In essence, tofurkey is faux turkey (for those of you who don't know, *faux* is the French word for ridiculous). It's a loaf made of tofu and filled with a stuffing made from grains, broth, herbs and spices.

As someone who is always trying to eat healthier, I picked one up for the holidays and eagerly placed it in the oven just as my guests began to arrive. I poured some cocktails as we engaged in conversation and noshed on hors d'oeuvres.

At the appointed time, we all moved to the kitchen and I removed the tofurkey from the oven. It glistened as I lifted it from the roasting pan and onto my carving board. One of my friends from France looked over my shoulder and, in a voice that could only be described as awe, whispered, *"Il a l'air d'un tas de merde d'éléphant"* (which I'm sure is the French term for "It looks delectably delicious").

We filled up our plates and took our seats around the table. After a toast and a blessing, we dug in.

After our first bite of tofurkey we all stopped and looked at each other.

Then we spat it out and reached for our glasses of wine.

It wasn't delectably delicious. At least as a tom turkey. Not even close.

Perhaps if they called it *Glorytree's Big Hunk O' Tofu* or even *Morning Farm's Self-Basting Thanksgiving Wad* it might've tasted better because we wouldn't have been expecting the taste of roast turkey on our palates.

Because here's the deal for me. I love vegetarian food, and I make it often. But I love it on its own terms. The minute someone tries to create something that it clearly is not (i.e. imitation turkey, hot dogs, bacon, etc.), I'm immediately put off because I know that a tofu dog will resemble a real Coney Island dog as much as snowman resembles a lawnmower.

So yes, fill my plate with real vegetarian ingredients and you can count on me to be back for seconds. But please leave the tofurkey in the grocer's cooler and pick up a real tom turkey for the holidays.

Sure, you might not hear someone gushing, *"Il a l'air d'un tas de merde d'éléphant"* over your shoulder, but I guarantee your guests will love you for it.

Now here are three typical questions that I often get asked as we approach the holidays.

How long can I keep a frozen turkey in my freezer?

During the holidays people often have more than one frozen turkey lying around. Perhaps they wanted to take advantage of a good sale or received a company turkey as a gift after they'd already purchased one. At the risk of having turkey every night from Thanksgiving to Presidents' Day, one must store the extras. If you have room, and your freezer is cold (as in 0 degrees) you can safely store a frozen turkey indefinitely. However, just because it's safe to store a frozen turkey until the cows come home, that doesn't mean that it's good to do so. If the texture or taste of the turkey is important to you, then it would be best to cook it within a year. If taste and texture are not important to you, then I would forgo the cost of buying a turkey and would freeze a chunk of Styrofoam instead. It's cheaper and available year round. Just be sure to make plenty of gravy.

I have a small kitchen, should I make my turkey or roast a day ahead of time?

If you're like many of us, your kitchen may not be conducive to creating a large feast, especially if you only have one oven. So it might sound like a good idea to cook your turkey or roast a day ahead of time and then reheat it after you've created the side dishes. While this may make sense in concept, it's not the best option. I reverse things and cook my side dishes a day ahead, then wrap them tightly and refrigerate them. The next day I cook the turkey or roast and they're done, I tent with foil and let it rest for 15 to 30 minutes. While the turkey or roast rest, I would put my sides in the oven to reheat. The texture of the turkey or roast will be far better than if you prepared it a day ahead of time. Besides, if you made enough, you'll have plenty of opportunity to delve into the leftovers, so why start your signature meal off with leftovers?

Can I make gravy without pan drippings?

I used to make gravy from pan drippings. Cookbooks are loaded with recipes for great pan gravies. It takes time, it's messy and you could end up with lumpy gravy. So, can you make gravy without the drippings? Absolutely! And although it's not as traditional as if you made it from the drippings, this recipe is downright delish. Oh, and it'll only take you 5 minutes to make it.

• EASIEST 'PAN' GRAVY MINUS THE DRIPPINGS •

I rarely make gravy from scratch anymore. I just don't have the time. So here's my go to recipe for gravy. With a jar of Better than Bouillon in the fridge, I can whip this up in 5 minutes. And it tastes pretty darn good, as well!

INGREDIENTS
- 2 cups turkey, chicken or beef broth made from soup base (or canned broth)
- 2 tablespoons cornstarch
- 2 tablespoons water

DIRECTIONS
1. Bring broth to a simmer in a small sauce pan. In a small bowl, stir cornstarch into the water until well combined.

2. Slowly stir the cornstarch mixture into the both until it reaches the desired consistency.

Makes 2 cups.

CHAPTER 59

EXCUSE ME WHILE I CHILL SOME WINE AND TAKE A FEW MOMENTS TO 'TEBOW'

If you've followed football over the past decade, you probably remember a phenomenon that sports pundits and fans alike labeled "Tebowing."

For those of you who've had better things to do than watch a multi-billion dollar industry amass another multi-billion dollars each fall, let me explain:

Tim Tebow was a former Denver Bronco and New York Jet quarterback who once led the Florida Gators to glory. At times, he chose to thank God for his success on the field by falling to one knee in prayer. Folks called this "Tebowing."

But hey, God and sports are not a new phenomenon. Remember that classic movie *Chariots of Fire*?

I've been a football fan since I was old enough to change channels on the TV. I can remember more than a few players expressing their thanks to the "Man Upstairs" on the field. I saw and heard many in the 60's "testify." I remember several players who flashed "Jesus One Way" signs in the 70's.

And Tebow wasn't the first player to drop to a knee to give honor to God after a good play. Heck, when I was in college in south Florida there were a number of the invincible and undefeated Miami Dolphins who attended bible studies at my alma mater and were not ashamed about doing so (can you say "Captain Crunch Mike Kolen"?)

Or how 'bout all those place kickers through the years whose names end in vowels crossing themselves before a field goal attempt?

And what's up with that wild-haired Polamalu fellah that used to play for the Steelers. His spiritual commitment would give some desert monks a run for their money.

Okay. Let me get to my point.

I would never think about asking any of them to stop doing these things even if I may not completely understand it all. Because I know that their faith drives them and it makes them who they are. To take that away or seek to diminish it would be robbing them of their inspiration.

So I say let Tebow or any other faith-filled sportsperson take a knee, whether Christian, Muslim or Jew. It's who they are. At least they realize that their talent, somehow, is a gift that's been entrusted to them.

But enough about sports. Let's move on to culinary excellence.

I've met more than a few great chefs over the past 30 years. Most were very thoughtful and gracious. I also worked with some who wouldn't take a knee for anything, not even to wipe up a spill. Their egos were so large one had to wonder how there'd be enough room in the kitchen for a decent skillet, let alone another chef.

For me, culinary expertise is a gift just like any talent. The ability to taste, tweak, or cook is all on loan. Those of us so blessed are responsible to hone it. But some chefs don't feel that way. To them their talent is purely self-induced and self-constructed and not a gift to be developed and honed. That way of thinking leads to ego inflation.

But like I said, all great chefs aren't like that.

I've met some who understand that their talent with a skillet, olive oil, onions and garlic is a gift. And they're humbled by that fact.

I hope to count myself among their number.

So if my next meal pleases the palates of my guests? Perhaps you just might catch a glimpse of me "Tebowing" in the darkness of my pantry. Because being thankful for whatever talent I might have is something I will strive for.

A few days ago we celebrated Thanksgiving. I know Who I gave thanks to. I'm trying to gain some perspective on the whole "talent thing" and Who exactly deserves credit. I think I'm starting to get it.

And if I ever start to slip? I just put Lucinda William's song *Blessed* in my stereo. Cooking with that incredible song in the background helps put things in perspective.

Now...which one of us will plate and who will say grace?

CHAPTER 60

LOVE ME. HATE ME. BUT PLEASE DON'T TOLERATE ME

Okay. I know this is a cookbook of sorts. But we need to talk.

First, let me top off your glass of Merlot. Say "when".

Good. Now, here's the deal.

I imagine I must've lost some readers with my holiday chapters.

But I find it hard to believe it was because my holiday tips offended them. Heck, if it was my left-of-decorum sense of humor that offended them, I'm sure they would've turned heel several chapters ago.

No. I think it was because I alluded to the sports phenomenon called "Tebowing".

In other words, I dragged God into my blog and now into this book.

Some folks appreciated it. Some folks were silent. But it appears that some folks were pretty upset. Why? As one e-mail expressed it, by reflecting on a highly successful quarterback offering my support for his expression of faith, I wasn't being, well, very "tolerant".

You've seen the bumper stickers. The ones that proclaim tolerance with the stylized 'Coexist' representing different religious beliefs. I was behind a car sporting one such bumper sticker in the parking lot of Target just this past weekend. But the driver must've used up all of her tolerance and coexistence at a previous store, 'cuz when a white Kia Rio with two missing hubcaps scooted into the parking place that she was obviously coveting, she rolled down her window and yelled something that vaguely sounded like "You muffin shucker!"

So much for, um, tolerance.

You see, I don't like the words "tolerance" or even its cousin, "tolerate".

Why do I dislike these seemingly pacifying words? Because tolerance and tolerate seem to infer that you are "putting up with something that you'd rather not have to".

In other words, you don't like something, so, to be a good sport or citizen, you have to just take a deep breath, suck it up, roll your eyes, and tolerate it.

Not me.

I have zero tolerance for "toleration". Or what I would call The Tolerance Principle.

Let me explain. I may like something or dislike something. If I do, I will let you know. I may agree or disagree with you. But, again, I will let you know.

However, like or dislike, agree or disagree, if what you espouse is held in conviction, I can respect it. But you can bet your $3 bumper sticker I won't simply "tolerate" it.

The Tolerance Principle particularly raises its ugly head during December when many folks shy away from expressing their deeply held beliefs lest they offend someone. So, whether it's a big wig corporation, the bubbly cashier at the local market, or the guy ensconced on the bar stool next to yours, many feel they have to resort to non-offending euphemisms like "Season's Greetings". (Of course, whenever I hear the words "Seasons Greetings" I immediately think of the salutation one would say to a particularly attractive jar of cumin or nutmeg).

But back to many people's penchant to not offend. Here's my take.

Ditch the euphemisms and wish me whatever is important to you. Christmas? Hanukkah? Kwanzaa? Winter Solstice? Hey, I'll respect it. At least you hold onto a conviction.

For nearly a decade I lived in an Orthodox Jewish neighborhood. Throughout the year, I was exposed to examples of that deeply-held tradition as my neighbors celebrated their festivals and faith.

But I tell you what; I sure as heck didn't role my eyes and "tolerate" those overt religious displays that were so different from my own. Nope. Instead, I respected them. In fact, my neighbor and good friend Neil's love for his sacred tradition inspired me to fully embrace my own.

So...if someone's faith inspires them to do well by their neighbor, I'm not gonna tolerate it. I'm gonna celebrate it.

Okay, there you have it.

And now I'm gonna say it.

Merry Christmas, everyone.

Love it. Hate it. But for Christ's sake* please don't tolerate it.

Now...who's up for a little celebrating?

* (I don't mean to say this in a flippant way - He loved us too much to "tolerate" much of anything...)

CHAPTER 61

TEN MORE HOLIDAY KITCHEN SAFETY TIPS

I received so many responses from my Ten Holiday Kitchen Safety Tips when I first shared them at shows that I thought ten more would be apropos for the season. I was especially encouraged by an e-mail from one bjorn99 who suggested that I take my Ten Holiday Kitchen Safety Tips and go jump in a lake (an obvious Norse holiday folk euphemism for Merry Christmas).

So in the spirit of the season, I offer ten more. (And may you, bjorn99, enjoy 'the lake' as well!).

1. Refrigerate all foods labeled "Keep Refrigerated." I know this sounds like a no-brainer. But remember what happened when you ignored the label that said "Warning: Keep Away from Open Flame."? I bet the eyebrows you used to remember.

2. There's really no such thing as the "Three Second Rule". If you drop something on the floor, you need to wash and dry it thoroughly or just toss it. Even if no one saw you drop it (popularly known as the "Rule of Non-Observance").

3   If you're making salad for a large holiday crowd, spinning a couple of heads of torn lettuce in your Maytag dryer is a better idea in concept than it is in real life.

4. Make it a habit to check for a hot stovetop before you touch it. If you have an electric range there should be an indicator light. If you have a gas range, a visible flame is a pretty good indicator.

5. Just because Giada De Laurentiis looks oh-so-hot in the kitchen with those form-fitting low-cut outfits doesn't mean that you will, too. And yes, I'm talking to you Andy.

6. If you need to get something down from the top shelf, for goodness sake use a step stool. Shouting, "Hey, honey, come give me a boost" is not, and has never been, a good idea.

7. Water, grease, and scraps of food can make the floor slippery. If you spill something on the floor, clean it up immediately. I know, I know, the dog will get to it. Or not.

8. Never leave the kitchen when you have something on the stove. Even if you're tempted to step out for a minute because Cousin Billy is in the backyard yelling, "Hey, everybody! Come watch this. I've never been able to do this sober before!"

9. If, while you're cooking, someone is constantly looking over your shoulder and saying, "That's not the way Great-Grandma Jenkins used to do it" then you need to turn and say "If Great-Grandma Jenkins did it a better way, then *why is she dead?"*

10. And finally, use cooking tools, utensils, and gadgets for their intended purposes. Even if your neighbor brags about how he once opened a stubborn jar of mayonnaise with a chef's knife and a hammer.

CHAPTER 62

IT'S A WONDERFUL LIFE, INDEED

Thanksgiving is past and you know what that means. Time to watch Jimmy Stewart and Donna Reed in the immortal classic *"It's a Wonderful Life"*. Yeah, yeah, I know the critics hated it, but the film has outlasted the critics.

I certainly enjoy it. Always have. It's not only thought provoking, it never fails to evoke memories of Christmases past. Fond memories all around.

I get the same type of feeling with a steaming cup of Chock Full O' Nuts coffee. Start up a potful and with one whiff I'm suddenly transported back to New York with its crowded nicotine-stained subways, Macy's glorious Christmas store windows, hot dog carts spewing steam, bustling automats, and traffic cops bundled up like the little kid in *"A Christmas Story"*. Sigh...those were the days.

Here's hoping your 12 days of Christmas are filled with joy and fond memories. It is, after all, a wonderful life.

And to help those memories along, here's a great recipe for mulled wine and some other heartwarming holiday beverages.

Thank you, Clarence. Hope you're enjoying those wings.

• TRADITIONAL MULLED WINE •

INGREDIENTS
1 bottles (750 ml) red wine

1/4 cup water

1/4 cup brown sugar

2 sticks cinnamon (or 2 teaspoons ground)

3 whole cloves

1 teaspoons ground nutmeg

1 bay leaf

1 orange, zested and squeezed (reserve juice)

DIRECTIONS
Bring the water to a boil in a dutch oven and add the sugar, cinnamon, cloves, nutmeg and bay leaf. Return to a slow boil and cook for 5 minutes, stirring to dissolve the sugar. Remove from heat and add the wine, orange juice, and orange zest. Warm over low heat (do not boil) for 30 minutes. Strain and pour into 6 stemmed glass mugs.

• HOT BUTTERED RUM •

INGREDIENTS

1 cup packed dark brown sugar

3/4 cup (1 stick) unsalted butter, room temperature

1/3 cup honey

3/4 teaspoon ground cinnamon

1/2 teaspoon ground nutmeg

1/4 teaspoon ground cloves

Pinch kosher salt

1 cup spiced rum

3 cups boiling water

6 sticks cinnamon, for garnish

DIRECTIONS

I a large bowl, combine the brown sugar, butter, honey, cinnamon, nutmeg, cloves, and salt. Mix with a hand blender until smooth. Transfer the mixture to an 8-cup Pyrex measuring cup (or a large bowl). Add the rum and then the boiling water. Stir until the butter mixture dissolves. Divide the buttered rum among 6 mugs. Garnish with the cinnamon sticks and serve.

• TRADITIONAL BOURBON HOT TODDY •

INGREDIENTS

1 oz (2 tablespoons) bourbon

1 tablespoon honey

2 teaspoons fresh lemon juice

1/4 cup boiling-hot water

DIRECTIONS

Put bourbon, honey, and lemon juice in a 6-ounce mug. Top off with hot water and stir until honey is dissolved. Makes one serving.

• TRADITIONAL IRISH COFFEE •

INGREDIENTS

1 cup freshly brewed hot coffee

1 tablespoon brown sugar

1 jigger Irish whiskey (1-1/2 ounces)

Heavy cream, slightly whipped, canned whipped cream

DIRECTIONS

Fill a stemmed glass mug (or regular mug) with hot water to preheat it, pour out the water. Pour piping hot coffee into warmed glass until it's about 3/4 full. Add the brown sugar and stir until dissolved. Stir in the Irish whiskey. Pour the whipped heavy cream gently over back of spoon, or add a dollop of canned whipped cream. Serve hot.

CHAPTER 63

A FINAL WORD ABOUT FOOD. WELL, MAYBE MORE THAN ONE

_____

Here ends yet another cookbook. Hopefully you had as much fun reading it as I had writing it. I also hope that the tips, hints and recipes will encourage and inspire you to engage your own culinary muse. We can talk about cooking all day, but until we've called our loved ones to the table to enjoy a meal seasoned with love, laughter and joy, we will truly miss out.

So don your apron, march into the kitchen and throw open the cupboards to see what you have. Then pour a glass of wine, fire up the stove, and let the improvisation begin.

Bon appétit!

Index

SALMON

Grilled Salmon with Garlic-Lemon Sauce, 143
No-Cook Sauce for Sautéed Fish, 193
Salmon Chowder, 197
Sautéed Salmon with a Pan Sauce, 192

SAUCES

Apricot Glaze, 219
Basic Pan Sauce Chicken, Pork, Beef
  or Fish, 192
Brown Sugar and Mustard Glaze, 219
Caribbean Dressing for Roasted
  Vegetables, 107
Chao Sauce for Lo Mein, 189
Decadent Dessert Sauce, 194
Easiest Pan Gravy Minus the Drippings, 225
Honey Soy Glaze, 219
hot or spicy sauce or salad dressing
  remedy, 61
Italian Style Dressing for Roasted
  Vegetables, 106
lumpy gravy remedy, 61
Mango – Avocado Salsa, 89
Maple Syrup and Mustard Glaze, 219
Middle Eastern Dressing for Roasted
  Vegetables, 106
No Cook Sauce for Chicken, Pork, Beef
  or Fish, 193
Oriental Dressing for Roasted Vegetables, 107
salty soup, stew or gravy remedy, 60
soy sauce and umami, 91
Shrimp Gravy for Grits, 186
Simple Aioli Sauce, 206

SHELLFISH

Bacon Wrapped Scallops, 75
Basic Refrigerator Soup, 201
Cajun Shrimp Mac & Cheese, 95
Crab Stuffed Sole, 64
Dublin Lawyer, 48
Garlicky Shrimp Pizza, 9
Greek Sautéed Shrimp, 171
Italian Sautéed Shrimp, 172
No Muss, No Fuss Lo Mein, 189
Quick Seafood Bisque, 132
Sautéed Cajun Shrimp, 169

Sautéed Spanish Shrimp, 170
Shrimp and Grits – My Way, 185
Shrimp Gravy, 186
Shrimp Mac & Cheese, 95
thawing shrimp, 35
Yucatan Shrimp, 3,4

SHRIMP

Basic Refrigerator Soup, 201
Cajun Shrimp Mac & Cheese, 95
Dublin Lawyer, 48
Garlicky Shrimp Pizza, 9
Greek Sautéed Shrimp, 171
Italian Sautéed Shrimp, 172
No Muss, No Fuss Lo Mein, 189
Quick Seafood Bisque, 132
Sautéed Cajun Shrimp, 169
Sautéed Spanish Shrimp, 170
Shrimp and Grits – My Way, 185
Shrimp Gravy, 186
Shrimp Mac & Cheese, 95
thawing shrimp, 35
Yucatan Shrimp, 3,4

SIDES

Boiled Carrots, 52
Boiled New Potatoes with Butter, 66
Broiled Tomatoes with Parmesan
  Cheese, 177
Caesar Salad, 208
Champ, 51
Colcannon, 44
Creamy Cole Slaw, 119
Easiest Black Beans, 156
Fried Plantains, 154
Garlic Smashed Potatoes, 220
Grits, 165
Mac & Cheese Variations, 94, 95
Old School Home Fries, 31
Sautéed Carrots in Honey Butter, 65
Spicy Oven Fries, 102
Steamed Green Beans, 220
Steamed White Rice, 155
Traditional Potato Salad, 120

74043587R00141

Made in the USA
Columbia, SC
10 September 2019